Flying Scot

Ian and Sir Wattie – Vet's inspection. Badminton 1986.

Flying Scot

STARK

IAN and JENNY STARK

PELHAM BOOKS

PELHAM BOOKS

Published by the Penguin Group
27 Wrights Lane, London W8 5TZ, England
Viking Penguin Inc., 40 West 23rd Street, New York, New York 10010, USA
Penguin Books Australia Ltd, Ringwood, Victoria, Australia
Penguin Books Canada Ltd, 2801 John Street, Markham, Ontario, Canada L3R 1B4
Penguin Books (NZ) Ltd, 182–190 Wairau Road, Auckland 10, New Zealand

Penguin Books Ltd, Registered Offices: Harmondsworth, Middlesex, England

First published 1988

British Library Cataloguing in Publication Data
Stark, Ian
  Flying Scot.
  1. Stark, Ian   2. Three-day event
  (Horsemanship)——Scotland——Biography
  I. Title   II. Stark, Jenny
  798.2′4′0924   SF295.7

ISBN 0-7207-1769-8

Made and printed in Great Britain by Butler & Tanner Ltd, Frome

Typeset by Quorn Selective Repro Ltd, Loughborough, Leicestershire

Contents

ACKNOWLEDGEMENTS 7

1 EARLY DAYS 9

2 TURNING POINT 26

3 OLYMPIC SILVER 43

4 BURGHLEY 1985 55

5 WATTIE'S YEAR 64

6 ROBBIE'S FINALE 78

7 MORE TRAVELS 87

8 THE TAIL END 97

AFTERTHOUGHT 111

THE EQUINE STARS 119

INDEX 124

Photo Credits

The authors and publishers are grateful to the following for permission to reproduce photographs in this book: James Douglas page 109; Edinburgh Woollen Mill page 76; Equestrian Services Thorney page 98; Brian Hill frontispiece, pages 40, 68, 73, 77, 124; Kit Houghton pages 31, 45, 47, 50, 51, 59, 74, 85, 99, 100, 104 (bottom), 107, 112, 113, 114, 115; Susan Luczyc-Wyhowska page 28; Northamptonshire Newspapers Ltd page 117; Samantha Pease page 70; Phelps Photography page 103; Peter Rollinson page 19, 29. The photographs on pages 10, 11, 13, 16, 20, 23, 53, 57, 62, 94, 104 (top), and 108 are from the authors' collection.

Acknowledgements

A very special thank you to the following:

David and Alix Stevenson and the entire Edinburgh
Woollen Mill – without whose support there would
be no need for this book.

Granny Stark and Granny McAulay for their never
ending help with both horses and children.

Claire Davies for all her horsey and kiddy help and for
typing the manuscript.

All the owners and breeders of all the horses involved
over the years.

John Beaton of Pelham Books for all his encouragement
in getting this book finished.

All our friends and neighbours who are so long suffering
with their never ending help and support.

Barbara Slane-Fleming for putting up with me (Ian).

Finally to our four-legged friends without whom I (Ian)
would still be a civil servant!?!

1
Early Days

IAN GREW UP in the small town of Galashiels in the heart of the Scottish Borders. This area is a very rugby-orientated one, but if you threw a rugby ball at Ian he says he would be more likely to run away from it than with it. His family is completely non-horsey, except for a great grandfather who had a fruit and vegetable business which involved the use of a horse and cart. He has one brother, Derek, who is an avid racing fan but he doesn't ride.

It is really the fault of Ian's sister Linda that, at the age of ten, he had his first ride on a horse and that was more or less by chance. Linda had booked a lesson at the local stables which were run by Will Boyle and decided that she was too frightened to go after all. For some reason Ian took her place, thoroughly enjoyed himself, and was quite unabashed by all Linda's schoolfriends who were there too.

A week later, Ian was out playing with friends in Gala Hill Wood. Will Boyle's horses could be seen in the distance going out on one of their morning rides. Ian remembers clearly that he stood watching them and quite suddenly felt so excited about going out again too, that he ran all of two miles to get home – to scrounge the necessary cash from the 'old dear' to pay for his lesson. As usual, Ian's mum would give him the money he needed even though she probably couldn't afford to do so at the time. Mrs Stark brought up her children single-handed. Everyone who knows her also knows how hard she has worked in her life to try and get the best for her three children. Pearl, as she is called, must have been horrified that

Trying to part the waves! On holiday 1963.

OPPOSITE TOP Looking nervous on his first introduction to a pony. Summer 1962.

OPPOSITE BOTTOM Whitley Bay Beach, 1962.

Ian wanted to go out riding again and kept all her fingers crossed that this would just be a passing phase in her son's life. Cash in hand, Ian disappeared at the run again to the stables. He remembers sitting and waiting there for three hours until the next lot of horses went out. Pearl, meanwhile, had no idea what was in store for her. From that day, even on their annual family holiday, he had to find ponies or even donkeys on the beach to ride, and that was the last Pearl saw of Ian at weekends.

From then on Ian spent every moment of his weekends at Will Boyle's stables at Ladhope. His mum gave in to the horse craze and bought him a second-hand pair of jodhpurs. From 8am until 10pm on every possible free day, and after school as well Ian worked with

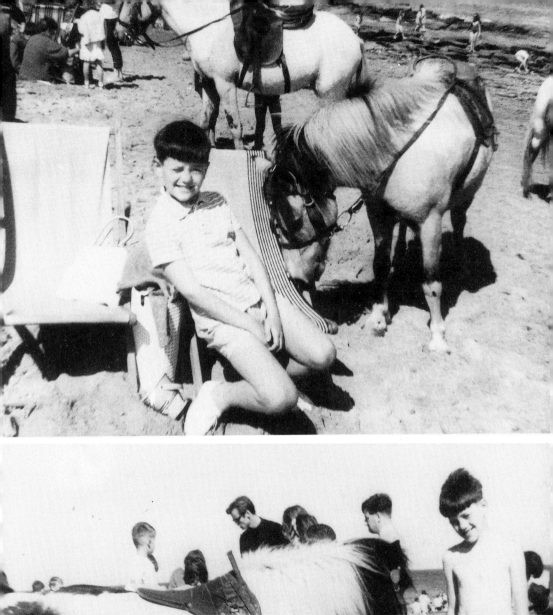

horses. He could not get this burning desire to ride out of his system with the result that his academic work went out of the window. Having been quite a promising pupil at primary school, by the time he got to Galashiels Academy for secondary education he was showing signs of having the worst attendance record of all of the pupils. He bullied his mum into writing sick notes for him to have days off especially in the summer. This was to prepare Will's horses for the local Border Festivals and Common Ridings.

Traditionally, every little Border town has a week in the summer revolving round the riding of their boundaries (known as the 'rideout'). A lot of people hire or borrow horses for these mounted equestrian occasions. Selkirk, our neighbouring town, in particular has anything up to six hundred riders when its turn comes. It has been called the biggest gathering of horses in Europe and is a stirring sight when they all leave the town at 7 o'clock in the morning. Hawick, another of our small towns, has a very strenuous hill ride to Mosspaul and back, a distance of eleven miles each way over the roughest and steepest Border hills, with many boggy, difficult areas to ride over. As well as the rideout there are races (the 'flapping') and the travelling fairs. Ian became so involved with these Common Ridings and was off school such a lot that one of his teachers became very concerned about his health. This was made worse by the fact that Pearl wrote so many notes to help him to be absent that she would forget what the last excuse was each time. The teacher took him aside and expressed her concern. Ian remembers standing there in front of his class with a completely straight face, telling her that he just wasn't a very strong child and that he suffered from 'flu' a lot. You can imagine the reaction of the others in the room, who knew fine what he was up to all the time!

From his early teens he was gaining tremendous experience riding a great variety of horses. Undoubtedly though, his favourite pony was one called Black Magic who belonged to Margaret Cranston of Broomhill, Selkirk. Margaret and her twin sister Anne were to play an important part in Ian's riding career. Margaret saw how keen Ian was to do more and more riding, and let him jump the mare at local shows. Black Magic's terrific, natural jumping ability over the five bar gates at Broomhill Farm probably

Ian's first jumping competition riding the late Margaret Cranston's outstanding pony, Black Magic. Selkirk Gymkhana 1967.

gave Ian his first taste of cross-country riding. Ian recalls that he 'used to just trot her at those big gates so that she could stop if she wanted to – but she never did and I almost fell off!' The other ponies which Ian rode at Will Boyle's were often when the boss was away. The boys who worked at the stables would catch them all up in rope halters and race bareback over jumps, frequently falling off but greatly improving their balance, if they could stay on!

They also larked around with an enormous ex-showjumper called Blue Horizon, who had a very bristly hogged mane. The game with him was to leap onto his back and canter round Will's field without a saddle or bridle. This was fun until the day, with Ian on board, the horse took on a huge metal gate out of the field. The rest of the boys had been sitting on the gate and all jumped off it hooting with laughter as the big horse got his eye on the obstacle and just kept going! Ian vividly remembers frantically sinking his fingernails into the non-existent mane as the horse sailed through the air and shot down a steep banking on the landing side. That was one stunt which got rather out of hand!

At the age of thirteen and still helping Will Boyle, Ian escorted rides of up to twenty or thirty people. They were all either beginners just learning to ride or regulars getting themselves fit for one of the Common Ridings. On one such occasion Ian was helping and closed a gate behind the riders when all the horses bolted. Loose horses ran amok, bodies were dotted all over the rough hill and lying around in the heather which they were crossing. One girl lay there for a long time with her knee badly smashed and they needed an ambulance to get her down off the hill to the town. The whole experience would have put many people off altogether. Not so for Ian. If anything, he became more hooked on the subject of horses because Will Boyle gave up his riding school business and when Ian was sixteen, Will bought smaller stables in Melrose. These were for liveries and many horses came in for dealing. Loads of them arrived from Ireland. Many of them were unbroken and some had manes to their knees. This is when Ian learned how to pull manes and tails, and plait. He could soon improve a horse's looks by the way it was clipped or plaited. Turning out a horse became second nature. However, Will refused to show Ian how he plaited tails, so Ian had to peek round a corner and watch him from a distance if he wanted to learn – this, of course, he did!

Young horses were backed quickly and ridden away, often while still tired after their journey from Ireland. Most of them did a summer's rideouts and Common Ridings, while others were sold on promptly. Will had hundreds of horses through his hands. One lady bought along a young horse she was trying to break but which kept bucking her off. Will lunged it and then held it while he legged Ian on board. Before they got it ridden away he was bucked off three times. Ian always remembers that Will received a bottle of whisky, while he got a 'thank you very much!' Horses that were still with Will in the winter became oated-up and produced for hunting. For Ian, as he was still at school, this meant a lot of riding exercise at weekends on over-fresh, often crazy horses. Will had a mean sense of humour at times and used to jump out from behind a certain tree with a lunge-whip in his hand. When his excited horses were going past they could be guaranteed to explode, reducing Will to hysterical laughter. You had to learn how to stay on. Ian must have done this well because Will soon gave him horses to hunt and to help break in for him. In return for this though, Ian had to do some work in Will's other business, a newsagent's shop. Funnily enough, he doesn't say much about that at all, except that there weren't even good horsey magazines to read!

One Saturday, Will took Ian out hunting on a young horse. After a very short time Will had to escort two of his lady owners home. He swopped horses with Ian first, to save the youngster and gave Ian the older horse, on the condition that Ian hacked it home. No sooner had he left than hounds started running like mad. The horse was thoroughbred and settled down to his top gear galloping and jumping, on and on. Ian forgot that he had at least six miles to hack home. He nearly had to carry the horse back. The vet was called in soon after his return and the verdict was 'exhaustion'. Ian had tried to sneak the horse back into its stable while Will was deep in conversation on the telephone. A bright, shiny, glossy looking animal had been turned into something looking twenty years old. Will was absolutely furious and the horse had to be rested for at least ten days. He never ever left Ian on his own out hunting again and always brought him home early after that incident!

Perhaps one of the first more exciting young horses which Ian had the chance to ride was a good looking thoroughbred mare which Will had bought at Doncaster sales. Ian thought that he had the measure of her, riding her quietly every day. He was furious when she bucked him off twice on a Saturday and twice on a Sunday, all in the one weekend. He is still wary of chestnuts to this day, but says that it taught him a lot! It annoyed him that she got rid of him so easily and the bruises lasted for a long time.

When Ian was eighteen and leaving school he was given the opportunity to ride and compete on a friend's horse. The friend was Jackie Rodger and the horse was called Glenmoidart.

As soon as Ian began competing, particularly in Pony Club and

15

Riding Club events, he realised what he wanted to do in life. All the experience gained beforehand seemed to show him the way. Glen was a big, quite heavy, grey gelding and was the first horse Ian rode in BHS novice events. Needless to say, Ian and Jackie are good friends to this day and Jackie letting Ian ride Glen really started something!

That first event was at Sunderland Hall, Galashiels, the home of a well-known local hunting family, the Scott-Plummers, and the regular venue for event and dressage meetings. He should actually have been third but there was a mistake with his cross-country timing and so he was not in the prize money. No one admitted that

Very first event, riding Jackie Rodger's Glenmoidart. Sunderland Hall 1972.

there had been a mix-up but they refunded his entry money which gave him some satisfaction and would probably not happen to him these days.

When Ian left school he signed on unemployed as he had no idea what he wanted to do. Two days later he was given a supposedly temporary job at the DHSS offices in his home town of Galashiels. This was the last place on earth where he wanted to work but he did so for the next ten years. Just as had happened at school, all his free time, holidays and sick leave were taken up by horses. The only difference now was that Ian had more say in what happened to each of the animals which he worked on because in some cases he owned a share in them with Jackie. He began to use up more and more time schooling other people's horses or clipping them during the winter. It must have been about this time that I first met Ian because he used to come and work horses in our indoor school at night after his work.

Perhaps I should say something here about my background. My father is a farmer and my mother, Jean McAulay, used to compete regularly and for years worked with local riding clubs. She has represented the Ettrick Forest Riders' Association at Stoneleigh and her work as an instructor earned her in 1975 the Leo Harris award from the British Horse Society. I started riding at an early age and when I was twenty I started a riding school at Dryden, my parents' home. My mother kept six ponies which were used by Riding for the Disabled and I decided that they might as well be made to work harder. My sister Catriona has now taken over the riding school.

Ian never used to know a thing about dressage until he rode a coloured horse called Indian Tonic, which belonged to Mrs Fanny Innes. This little chap took him by surprise, doing a good test at a Riding Club one-day event. He decided that from then on, to be a more successful competitor, he would have to 'crack this dressage carry on!' and not just go in to an arena hoping for the best. At this time he had two very good greys called Greyfriars Lass and Greyfriars Bobby. He learnt lots with them, eventing and show-jumping and was very successful. However, the mare was very tense in her dressage and nearly bucked him off in the middle of the arena at Fenton, once described as the 'Badminton of the North'. Fenton is near Wooler in Northumberland and sadly this event is no longer run. A great deal of its success was due to the work of the Joicey family. It was the first Open Intermediate Class in which Ian had ridden and he was trying out a slippery, new, dressage saddle. Her bad behaviour was just the final straw! He sold her into show-jumping and took himself back to the drawing board.

To improve his 'dressage lark' he went for some tuition. One of the people he went to was a local dressage judge, Mrs Joan Scott-Plummer, who owned a well-schooled German horse. He got to know her quite well when he stabled his horses for a while on her estate at Sunderland Hall, Galashiels. Very generously, she offered him some lessons on her imported dressage horse but it was rather a cumbersome animal and lazy to say the least. Ian got extremely exasperated with it and used some strong leg aids and language, whereupon Mrs Scott-Plummer, usually a quiet lady, yelled at him, 'Don't kick my horse!' and 'Why are you always kicking?' The lessons continued for a while but became known to Ian and his friends as the 'don't kick my horse' sessions.

After these, Ian went on to get more help from Mrs Jean McAulay, who was later to become his mother-in-law. As he was a member of the Ettrick Forest Riding Club team bound for regional finals, my mother summoned him to see how his flat work was going. 'I won't interfere with your jumping, Ian,' she used to say, 'but let me see this dreaded flat work!' My mother was determined that 'her' riding club team was going to do well 'down south'. Ian and I had ridden in one such team on a previous occasion. He was totally out of control on Glenmoidart and I overfaced a fat fell pony that we called 'Roger the Lodger'. That team had fizzled out! 'Mrs Mac' was not about to let that happen a second time. Ian brought a horse to her for schooling called Gallant Lad belonging to Bob Cranston, father of the twin sisters, Anne and Margaret Cranston. Now this thoroughbred did not like flat work – or jumping

OPPOSITE TOP Ian on Mrs Fanny Innes' Indian Tonic at a Riding Club team event – this was the horse that changed Ian's views about dressage.

OPPOSITE BOTTOM Ian on Greyfriars Lass, Novice Horse Trials at Corbridge 1974.

Ian on Greyfriars Lass (nearest camera) in pairs hunter trials with Tony Hogarth on Master Adam. Greenhill, Selkirk, 1974.

particularly. He was nothing like his name suggested. My mother shook her head sadly. She would hate to admit it but she introduced Ian to that gadget called draw reins hoping by doing so that the team could pull off a win at Stoneleigh! It turned out to be a rare occurrence of Ian having a stop on the cross-country so he was not amused.

My mother is a stern taskmaster who is not given to handing out unwarranted compliments but at about this time she said of Ian that 'there is no substitute for his natural talent'.

For several years Ian was a really staunch member of the Ettrick Forest Riding Club going to all their competitions and featuring in all their teams. At one point I twisted his arm to go on the fund-raising committee for them. We ran a couple of very good barn dances, in the indoor school at Dryden, for about a thousand people. That was until my father became too nervous about his hay sheds going on fire, for these to continue. When we started rather warily going out together we must have had more lunch dates than

Ian competing in his first CCI at Wylye on Woodside Dreamer in 1979.

any other couple. Neither of us had any spare time in the evenings to go out, so it was mid-day dating as far as we were concerned. On one rare occasion we were to go out on a Friday night to see the film, *One Flew Over the Cuckoo's Nest*. I sat waiting for a very, very long time then went on to the movie on my own. Ian was just out looking at horses for friends called Jean Slater and Errol Keay. He forgot to mention this was on the agenda but, I thought to myself, 'You might as well start the way you mean to continue,' and let's face it, 'the leopard doesn't change it's spots!' I was quite reasonable and calm in view of the circumstances!

In 1978 Ian was riding a young mare called Woodside Dreamer which he decided to enter at Wylye novice three-day-event. He and Jackie Rodger jointly owned her, and, as they set off to that competition I wonder if they realised that Ian was just putting his toe on a ladder which he would want to climb to the very top. With his usual determination he rode 'Corrie' as he called her into eighth place. He then returned to Wylye the following year, 1979, with the same horse and came eleventh in the Standard section. He was absolutely fired with inspiration on his return home and thought that everything was set fair for Badminton the next year. But . . . .

By this time we had been living together for some months to see if we enjoyed more of each other's company than lunch dates. Much to all the parents' relief we got married in November 1979 and amongst the possessions which I took with me to Haughhead, where we live, was an aggressive Highland pony cross by the name of Fergus of Dryden. He took one look at Corrie and decided to kick her into the middle of next week. He did this with great accuracy and nearly broke her hock. She was lame for a very long time. We may have been newly-weds but were nearly newly-divorced as a result. I can tell you, the air was blue! When Ian worked in the office a great friend and fellow work mate called Barbara Laub used to tease him about his temper and say, 'Look out folks, its one of those days, light the blue touch paper and stand back!' Well, when Fergus kicked Corrie I had to stand about half a mile back.

Sadly, although Woodside Dreamer evented again, she never took Ian back to a three-day event. Ian was desperate to ride at that level but just did not have the horses. Woodside Dreamer has now retired to stud, at first with Sheila Mardon at Inverurie and now with Sam Barr in Gloucestershire.

I also took to our marital home about six young Highland ponies which I had to break and sell that year. We don't have much land where we stay and at that time the fences weren't in great shape either. The ponies did not help matters at all. They leant on and bashed their way through any piece of fencing which looked at all reasonable. They actively encouraged our other horses to behave like tanks as well. Each night when Ian came back from his work at the office, some more fence had gone. Let's just say it was fortunate that I got all the ponies backed and sold quite quickly otherwise . . . .

Not long after we moved into Haughhead I had to get used to the 'things must be done yesterday' feeling you get in Ian's company. Perhaps I am just as bad because our two children arrived in quick succession, with only fourteen months between them! Ian came to

Family life – Ian with Stephanie, Tim in the high chair and Kelly the dog. Haughhead 1982.

watch their arrivals in the world and said it was most amusing – 'two of the funniest days in my life,' he said. That's not what I was thinking but I did appreciate him being there at the time.

As well as starting our family life together rather smartly, we decided to make big alterations to our home and its surroundings. To my mother's absolute horror we bulldozed the old stables which were there and had some old trees whacked down which we thought blocked out the light to the house. We had some sectional loose boxes put up for us, and being us, were using them for horses before the concrete floors were in.

On one particular evening after his work, Ian dashed out in his usual fashion to jump a horse in the half-dark. This horse was really supposed to be preparing for point-to-pointing but Ian thought it would benefit from some schooling over fixed fences. Our friend, Jackie, had just built him some new, very solid post and rails (to replace those utterly demolished by Highland ponies). I looked out of the bedroom window to see Ian galloping around like a maniac on 'Charlie Riddell-Webster' as we called the racing prospect (we'd named him after his owner). In a howling wind and lashing rain he proceeded to turn upside down over a large fence at the bottom of the garden and fall, face first, into a deep pool of floodwater. I thought he'd taken total leave of his senses. It was so dark by this time it was difficult to see if he was even on his feet. Charlie had galloped off into the darkness. I stood at the window as if hypnotized to see what the next part of the action would be. Slowly a figure crawled up the garden path and banged on the back door. When I opened it, a blood-stained and soaking wet Ian was sitting on the garden bench. 'You can't come in like that!' I said, 'You'll frighten the children,' who were probably nearly drowning in their bath anyway. This was where the two wee souls had been abandoned when all the dramas were going on outside. To finish that story, I fished the kids out of the bath and left them with my mother, who, by now, had decided that her son-in-law was bonkers anyway, and I took him off to the hospital in case his nose or jaw was broken. It wasn't, but I really don't know how. I've seen Ian compete all over the world now but never seen him have a fall like that one. Perhaps many of the worst falls are whilst schooling and not necessarily in the heat of a competition.

At this stage, Ian did do some more point-to-pointing as well but never really with the enjoyment or success of his eventing. He rode a chestnut mare called Nobilin for Bill Hughes at Galashiels. The main problems as I could see them were that the owner/trainer i.e. Bill, and the jockey i.e. Mr Stark, could not agree on the mare's diet. Bill insisted on trying to keep her strength up with enormous haynets. The jockey was always protesting that it wasn't supposed to be a barrel race! Also, Ian would not do what his owner was telling him. Bill's instructions were, 'to sit nice and quietly at the back of the race for the first circuit'. We all stood watching the start with great excitement, fivers on the 'fat one'. The flag went up and out shot Nobilin like a bullet from a gun. Totally out of control, Ian led over the first fence getting sworn at by the other jockeys for going so fast. Later, perhaps fortunately, he got lost in the fog. Bill said patiently that there was always another day and we all trooped home. Ian said that it was a terrifying experience sitting in the middle of a herd of horses all rising up beside him and in front of him like a wave. He prefers a clear view of his fences and is too competitive to sit behind the others! This sport was not going to take over from eventing.

2
Turning Point

FOR US, IN MANY ways, the year 1982 brought the most important turning point in Ian's career. About two years after we were married Ian was put onto flexi-time at his work. I have never seen just such flexible hours. 9.30 in the morning until 3 in the afternoon, with a two-hour lunch break, would try any employer's patience. Eventually I couldn't stand it any more because he was complaining so much about his job. He used to 'phone in and say the road was too badly blocked for him to get into the office, and we had only half an inch of snow. Or, holding his nose so that it sounded as though he had a terrible cold, he would pretend to be in bed. I was rushing around feeding horses in the stables and changing babies' nappies in the house. These two jobs always seemed to need to be done at the same time and so I just said to him that I didn't really care if he left his work because there seemed to be so much to do at home. To be fair, it did take him five minutes to take in what I'd just said but I didn't have to repeat it! His seniors at the DHSS couldn't believe their ears when he handed in his notice. They had become so used to him not being there that they were quite taken aback when he formalised the situation after ten years!

Looking back it was probably the right decision at the right time. We were both working really hard and Ian was eventing more and more. The main break we had been waiting for came. Oxford Blue (Robbie) and Sir Wattie came to stay with us. Although Ian had gained a tremendous reputation for sympathetically and systematically training and producing young or difficult horses, the arrival in our yard of these two six-year-old geldings, both of whom showed great potential, was very exciting. It was the best challenge Ian had had in his career with horses so far.

Oxford Blue was bred up in Aberdeenshire by two ladies called Mrs Norah Machattie and Miss Liz Davidson. His dam was a mare called Blue and Norah sat up all night with Robbie when he was born. Robbie was sired by Andrew Spence's Cagirama, the sire of many point-to-pointers, hunters and show horses in Scotland.

One evening Ian received a garbled 'phone call from Norah saying that Liz was very keen to buy Robbie back from Mrs Pollyann Lochore, to whom they had sold him as a three-year-old. Pollyann has represented Britain in the past and is also based in the North. The horse, now six, was about to go on the market and 'How did Ian feel about riding him?' asked Norah. Rather than lose touch with the horse Liz wanted to own him again and hoped she could see him take his eventing a bit further. Polly had started him carefully in novice events to give him experience and had various young horses for sale.

Ian and I went to see Robbie perform in the Working Hunter Class at the Royal Highland Show at Ingliston. He came sixth, looked very nice and jumped clear but Ian was privately thinking that the horse 'looked extremely novicey and hairy!' Ian tried him on the flat and liked what he felt but wondered what he would think over some jumps. We searched for the practice jump and found one which fourteen twos were flying backwards and forwards over. We had to put it down a lot as it was about five feet high and Ian felt nervous just looking at it. The juniors all giggled as he popped Robbie over a minute cross-pole and said, 'thank you all very much,' patting the horse and walking him back to an excited Liz and Norah. Ian knew then that Robbie didn't have a big jump but he obviously had a quiet temperament and seemed fairly willing. 'Do you think he'll be fast enough?' he kept asking as we drove home having made the arrangements to take the horse on. Liz bought Robbie back for Ian to ride the day before the advertisement came out in the *Scottish Farmer*!

Wattie came to stay with us under rather different

Sir Wattie as a foal.

circumstances. We had met him several times before as he is rather a character. Bill Hughes was breaking him in for the two ladies who then owned him, Mrs Susan Luczyc-Wyhowska and Dame Jean Maxwell-Scott. Dame Jean and Mrs Luczyc-Wyhowska owned a roan mare called Rosie and when her hunting days were over they decided to breed from her. Wattie was the result and his sire was Bronze Hill, a local horse who has sired several good competition horses. He was named Sir Wattie after a Maxwell-Scott family name. Bill, who worked for Mrs Luczyc-Wyhowska, initially spoke to Ian about him riding the horse in four-year-old show classes. Wattie put paid to that idea by growing himself an angleberry the size of a man's fist, right where his girth was

Sir Wattie at his first event at Charterhall, near Duns, 1982.

supposed to be. He was off for at least six months while that was
sorted out.

As a five-year-old he had started hacking out along the roads
around Kelso and seemed fairly sensible. It was thought to be the
right time to introduce Wattie to the Riding Club classes held at
Dryden Indoor School. Here he would be able to work amongst
other young horses and start jumping in the safety of four walls.
Bill brought him along and Ian popped on his own saddle which
was probably just as well. As Ian climbed aboard, Wattie took a
deep breath, walked four steps and let Ian see what the rafters
looked like. It was only by the grace of God that the horse was still
there when Ian came down again. My mother was taking the

group at the time and ordered everyone else to stand still which they all did anyway because they were petrified just watching. Wattie continued his bucking fit for some time and Ian shouted, 'Open the doors and let me out of here!' because he was so worried someone else was going to get hurt. Just then Wattie simmered down a bit and the lesson continued. It took Ian the whole hour session before he could even dare to try a few steps of canter. He was exhausted by the time he came in for his supper and hoped Wattie was the same. After this incident we took the horse in for a fortnight to try and get him past this naughty phase. As Ian worked on the youngster he found him favouring a big fast trot or gallop and he showed a big promising jump. His pet hate was slow, dressage canter and it probably still is to this day. The horse was soon due to go home to Wooden, Kelso where he was only being ridden occasionally. This has never suited him because he always benefits from regular, hard, work and concentration! Bill and Ian had another of their serious chats about Wattie in the autumn of his five-year-old year. There was no doubt he was a bit of a handful and so it was gradually arranged that he came to us.

At this time Ian had been down to Badminton as a spectator a couple of times with friends. Working with Woodside Dreamer had been his nearest hope of competing there but she had by now gone by the wayside. Luckily for us, Shuna Mardon, Lorna Clarke's sister had taken the mare to breed from to her Quarter Horse stallion. Now, the green light for 'go' was shining again. Robbie and Wattie were soon showing themselves to have the consistent records and the potential needed for top eventing. That year, 1982, saw them come swiftly up through novice classes together. They were both second at Eglinton, both placed at Alnwick and both won at Dalmahoy Horse Trials. Coming to the end of that first autumn event season, Wattie threw a splint, and Robbie went on his own to Claughton Horse Trials in Lancashire. The course was so big there that Ian privately thought he would be eliminated and end Robbie's eventing career! However, they both

OPPOSITE Charlie Brown IV boldly through the water – Novice Championships Locko Park 1983.

moved on successfully up through the grades and 1983 saw them both into advanced classes and Ian quietly hoped then he would ride them both at Badminton one day. He ran them both at Bramham three-day-event in Yorkshire that summer. That was a lucky event for us and has many happy memories. Ian won on Wattie and was third on Robbie. It was shades of things to come. These two were always level-pegging and he loved riding them both for different reasons. The press always tried to get him to say that he preferred one to the other!

Ian returned to Bramham Horse Trials and won there three years in a row with different horses. The first year there was special though because he ran as the 'outsider', a position which he might never hold again. As seven-year-olds his horses were comparatively young and their ensuing success seemed to send the press wild. I will always think of it as the event which changed everything for us. There was no turning back. Luckily for us it was a relaxed family outing as well. We had the children with us and also our staunch friends Claire Davies and Anne Cranston to help us out. Claire supported us from the time she left school and has frequently been our lucky mascot at competitions. It seemed to be a weekend of marvellous weather with picnics and I wonder if any other event we have been at has been so easy-going. We bought videos of both horses over the three days and were to watch them over and over again. Winning this event gave Ian a thrill which he had only experienced once before when learning to fly a plane! Ian is crazy about flying and if funds permitted he would still be flying; it is something he hopes he can take up again in due course.

We got home to piles of fan mail for Ian and stacks of 'Well Done' cards. Interviews with newspapers, articles by all sorts of journalists, requests to do talks and speeches at dinners – all these seemed to flood in. The children were still young enough to be blissfully unaware of their father's overnight fame: it took some getting used to. Ian seemed to take it in his stride while I died a thousand deaths. Every time a camera zoomed in Ian waved and grinned. The funniest article must have been in one of the Glasgow papers where I was written up as the aggressive, pushy wife who supposedly said in an interview, 'I always knew that he could do it!'

Charlie Brown IV 'making chips' at Locko 1983.

Another one printed an article on Ian saying that he achieved success with the help of hedgehog skins under the saddle. Joking apart Ian expected a 'phone call any minute from the BHS or the FEI to query these allegations and we soon learned not to give everyone interviews and had enough of being misquoted. Some weeks went by before things quietened down a little. Ian made some of his entries for the autumn events which loomed ahead and mentioned competing abroad on some BHS entry form and put in a couple of ticks beside one or two foreign names, never thinking any more about it.

One afternoon, completely out of the blue, a lady rang from Pedens International horse transport. I presumed she must have rung the wrong number and I went back to the washing machine. The 'phone rang again. Ian answered it this time, getting suspicious. 'This is Lorna Clarke here,' the voice said, 'I'm your chef d'equipe for Achselschwang.' The 'phone call was brief and in her slightly clipped way she soon rang off. We burst out laughing. Where had she just said – somewhere in Germany?' Arrangements had to be made extremely quickly and Wattie prepared for what was to be a very long, tiring journey, first of all to Yorkshire, where we met Liz and Alwyn Kershaw, who have been kind to us ever since that crazy trip! We stay with them often for events and on one occasion the children were sick all over Liz's kitchen floor, while on another, I took such a wild attack of chickenpox that Liz swore she would burn the bedclothes to rid her house of plague! They run a farm and Liz is a regular competitor in events up and down the country.

We drove away from Yorkshire in Liz's smart new lorry to Newbury to meet up with the Clarkes. Alwyn had decided to fly out to Munich with a friend, perhaps a wise choice in view of the distance we had to cover. Having teamed up with Lorna and crossed over to Europe at Dover we just appeared to drive and drive and drive. The journey seemed to take forever. The funniest part was that by some unspoken agreement Lorna and Ian took over Liz's lorry and didn't allow her to drive at all! Normally her horsebox travelled around sedately, but on this occasion it was battered across Europe like there was no tomorrow. It was only allowed a breather at custom posts. Every time Liz said that she could drive for a turn, Ian and Lorna said in chorus, 'Oh, I'm not tired!' and one of them would leap back into the driver's seat. I thought Liz showed she was a great sport to allow complete strangers to do this – especially as Lorna was always hanging her head, an arm or even a leg, out of the window to stay awake while she was driving during the night! When Alwyn met up with us at Achselschwang he spent a long time under the bonnet of the lorry.

Normally his pride and joy, he was very aware that the engine was now fully run in which it had not been before.

Lorna had been out to this German event previously and very kindly organised for us all to stay with her friends, Barbara and Theo Steinler. Any spare time at the event she used up by taking us off to see places of interest and do things, so that it was an educational trip as well. We ended up at the Munich Beer Festival one night, which was an experience in itself! To the 'oom-pa-pa' music, we demolished half roast chickens and two pint mugs of beer. Whether it was a good idea or not to go up on a Big Wheel after that was a matter of personal choice – a strong case of mind over matter!

The event seemed to be over all too quickly leaving us with memories of the excellent German hospitality we had received during our stay. The team had won, but not by much. The three of them had four fences in hand as they went forward to the show-jumping phase. Lorna will always remember it as the three-day event where she had five fences down! Liz did a lovely clear round on Just the Thing. As Ian went in for his turn Lorna said grimly, 'If you have one down you lose the lead, if you have two down we lose the team.' Ian did hit two fences, but as there were only two clears in the whole day, our team of Taimur, Just the Thing and Sir Wattie held on to their lead. The organisation at Achselchwang was outstanding in that the final results were released in minutes and the trophies were presented, already engraved with the horses' names on them. It was a good excuse to be introduced to Schnapps by our kind German hosts, sorry to see us set off on our long trek back. Lorna's popularity as an international competitor is second to none and thank goodness she spoke enough German to look after us all in some tricky situations!

The drive home seemed almost longer than the one there and there wasn't the incentive of an event ahead. I was keen to get back though as Tim, two years old at the time, had been ill and not eating while we were away. One of our 'phone calls home had been an upsetting one as Granny sounded very worried about him. She had taken him to the doctor who said he was pining for his mummy! We kept on bashing northwards and we were desperately tired as we crawled up the last leg of the journey to Scotland. In the thirty-six hours it took us to get from Germany to Scotland our groom, Susan McGlashan, managed to sleep the entire trip, even when a suitcase fell on her head!

As soon as we got home the first thing Ian did was to open all the letters which had arrived in our absence. The rest of us were rather disconsolately cleaning the mountain of mess out of the lorry – probably the worst job after an event is over. A yell from the kitchen window made us turn our heads. 'Start packing!' Ian shouted, 'we're going to Boekeolo in Holland next week, whoopee!' I just looked in disbelief. When you feel really tired you could just cry sometimes.

Anyway we were soon to be off again. Or should I say, Ian set off with someone else to help. This time I thought I would miss out on the 'incredible journey' theme and fly out to join him. I had to catch a train across Holland but that did not worry me half as much as getting a rest did. The financial side of life was also becoming a nagging worry at the back of my mind. Many of the other riders going out to Boekeolo seemed to be sponsored and as Ian appeared to be developing a taste for foreign travel the future promised to be expensive. I knew that if we were going to be away a lot then things at home would suffer and my heart sank. It was a horrible feeling and put a lot of strain between us, especially when Ian's success was taking him high onto the crest of a wave.

Ian drove off in high spirits with Oxford Blue in our clapped-out old lorry. A few days later I caught the necessary flights and trains out to Boekeolo and made my way into the event which seemed quite easy to find. The first person I bumped into was Lorna who surprised me by immediately asking if Oxford Blue was really for sale. Many people were interested in Robbie at that time and at the end of the season perhaps riders are already looking ahead to another year, particularly if their horses have gone unsound. Once, Lars Sederholm flew up to Edinburgh with a client to try Robbie and they turned him down due to his lack of show-jumping talent – something Ian and Lars can still have a chuckle about. Just then, when money was scarce, the whole subject of selling Robbie seemed imminently important. Basically Liz did not want to sell the horse though and looking at all the things he has done for Ian now, thank goodness he didn't persuade her to. The final choice was always to be left up to him!

I was wandering around looking for Ian when a voice behind me said 'Have an eel'. Eel sandwiches seemed to be the in-thing, everyone ate them. Certain things always remind you of certain places but I never expected those to remind me of Holland!

Boekeolo was a far bigger event than Achselschwang in that many more of the 'big' names were riding there. Ian had had an exciting start getting out there in the first place by being late for the ferry at Hull and nearly missing it. The poor old Bedford lorry boiled over and the radiator cracked meaning that Ian had to stop and fill up with water every half hour. Robbie had a mild colic on arrival but very fortunately he recovered in twenty-four hours. Possibly it was due to our lack of knowledge at the time about cutting back hard feeding in preparation for long journeys. Ian was pleasantly surprised to be told that he was in the team with Lucinda Green on Village Gossip, Tiny Clapham on Jet Set, and Lizzie Purbrick on The Grousebeater. Ian felt that at last he was 'in with all the stars', especially when Richard Meade was riding as an individual on Andeguy. Charles Harrison, Chef d'Equipe, and Marjorie Comerford were keeping everyone right and Ian was very grateful to them for all their advice throughout that trip. Ian has always felt that he can go to them for help and advice with any problems. Marjorie is a most popular and very successful international event rider. He was most encouraged that Robbie felt really well in spite of his initial hiccup on arrival, and, in fact, the vet at the ten minute halt on cross-country day said the horse was about the fittest he had seen all day.

Ian's memories of Boekeolo Horse Trials are the series of marvellous parties he went to; the hosts who looked after the riders so hospitably, and then the fact that he nearly blew it all on the cross-country itself! Galloping along in top gear he was so carried away with the wind whistling past his ears that he forgot about a sharp left hand turn and went straight past a gap in the hedge which they were all supposed to go through. Lady Hugh Russell was sitting watching in the well-known Mini Moke and I'm sure she must have nearly shouted at Ian or driven after him. Afterwards she asked him if he was galloping off to Enschede, the nearest big town! Show-jumping day brought out one of Robbie's best efforts, a clear round over the solidly built jumps which suited him. To Ian's delight the team won and Robbie was seventh individual, with Richard Meade jumping a copybook round to win on Andeguy. After it was all over, the rest of the Brits were held up in Holland for nearly a week by bad weather. By some fluke we were allowed to board the Hull ferry and got home on the Monday morning, quite unaware that all the others were left behind!

Ian was thrilled when he got home to find a letter saying that both Sir Wattie and Oxford Blue were on the long list for the 1984 Olympics in Los Angeles. It was a fantastic achievement in itself and Ian was very proud of both 'boys', knowing he would hate to have to make the decision of which one to take and never thinking for one minute that both his horses would actually travel out to America that summer.

The first and most important hurdle in the spring of 1984 was Badminton. His life-long ambition to ride there was now so nearly in his grasp, and the knowledge that if both horses went well they could perhaps be short-listed for the Olympics was another tremendous boost to his riding career. Lorna Clarke invited him down to stay at Newbury for the last few weeks before the great three-day event. At that time Lorna was based at Newbury but she now spends most of her time in Scotland. I stayed at home meanwhile with the kids and other horses that were in work. Very luckily for us the ever-reliable, conscientious Claire Davies was able to accompany Ian to look after his horses. We hoped that if they all made it to LA that Claire would be able to go too because if anyone deserved to go, she did. Claire came to us when she left school to work as groom, nanny and invaluable all-round help. She became like part of the family and still rides out every morning before her work.

Wattie was to be Ian's first ever ride round Badminton. How fitting it was then that the same partnership returned there to win two years later. The whole atmosphere of Badminton is difficult to describe and the feeling of excitement amongst the competitors is terrific. The house and park are quite magnificent and most of the horses are stabled in the old stable block where the hunt horses normally live. On the Thursday evening all the competitors and officials are invited by the Duke and Duchess of Beaufort to a cocktail party in Badminton House. We slept in our horse box and ate in the old kitchens in the house with the others and this all helped to create the special Badminton atmosphere.

Ian recalls that 'On that first ride I made so many mistakes and put Wattie wrong hundreds of times,' but the horse kept getting him out of scrapes. One of the worst moments to watch was at Horsens Bridge where, on landing, Wattie came down so low on his pasterns that I thought something in his legs would snap! Robbie however, scuttled round in his long-reined almost laid-back style, taking very little out of himself. It was his 'giving-just-enough' way of going, yet showing that he had stamina, that probably got him chosen as the preferred ride for the intense heat which lay ahead at the Olympics. Although generous, he has always taken as little out of himself as possible and this is an advantage when there is a hot climate to cope with as well.

That first Badminton for Ian was in many ways the most memorable one. For a start, he nearly couldn't compete due to a bad attack of food poisoning. Everyone thought he was suffering from nerves! I had to dash over to the Red Cross tent to extract some foul tasting medicine from them for Ian so that he could manage to ride the two horses on cross-country day. He had already been filmed by the BBC as a beginner riding at his first Badminton on the dressage day, I just hoped the cameras didn't catch him dosing himself with kaolin and morphine because the faces that followed would not have looked too good on film! Obviously before he set off on Wattie he was nervous but he looked forward to the challenges of the course. With hindsight, he learned a lot about the jumps and their various problems on this first ride with the result that Robbie benefitted as Ian set out for the second time. This was just as well as Liz Davidson had come all the way down from Aberdeen to spectate, her first and only time at Badminton, and the only three-day event she saw Robbie compete at. Perhaps the real reason why he did well on both horses was that

Ian's first Badminton rides, Sir Wattie and Oxford Blue, parading before Her Majesty The Queen, 1984.

just before the start of Phase A, on Wattie, Ian recognised a familiar face in the enormous crowd. It was Mrs Rowena Whitson (Charlie Brown's owner) wearing her lucky straw hat, just for Ian's benefit!

On the show-jumping Sunday morning Ian was shaking before the vetting. This is a nerve-racking time for any competitor and made much more intimidating by being held in the formal surroundings at the front of the big house itself with the Duke and members of the Royal Family watching, and a highly interested crowd, jam-packed behind railings. Both our horses looked fit and well so we had no need to worry, but it is still a great relief when the necessity is over.

Ian was edgy as the show-jumping itself drew nearer. This is his least favourite phase because so much can be lost in a matter of mere seconds. I knew there was something else bothering him and wondered what on earth it was. We wandered over to the stands to while away some time until the course was open for inspection. We seemed to drift from one saddler's tent to the next. Then he stopped in front of some red jackets. 'What do you think?' he asked me, holding one up for size. 'I did wait till after the vetting,' he said, almost apologetically. I just had to laugh. Ian always succumbs to his expensive taste in clothes! Whatever else, if he made it into this famous show-jumping arena, he was going to look the part.

Claire Davies and Sarah Campbell, our New Zealand help, were busy plaiting up and titivating the 'boys' and all the tack. They were not at all surprised that Ian bought himself his new jacket and are quite used to his spending sprees! Seeing that the horses looked absolutely immaculate Ian got himself ready too and we walked rather solemnly over to look at the course. It cheered him up tremendously that Lucinda came across to him, shook his hand and said, 'Well done, yesterday!' He felt that it was a very friendly gesture on her part when he hardly knew her at the time and Badminton was considered by many to be her own hunting ground as she has won the competition so many times.

Ian went in to show-jump Wattie first and ran early because his two rides were lying third and fourth before this phase. He knew one of them would drop down the order now but didn't know which it would be. It was Wattie who hit the white gate and he went down to sixth. Robbie went clear and it was the last time he did in a three-day event. Liz Davidson was thrilled to see him hold onto his third place and Ian couldn't believe the event was all over and both his horses had tried so well for him.

Well, we returned home and Ian had done it, ridden at Badminton and achieved his ambition. It came back to me that when we got married he had said he wanted to ride there – what I hadn't realised was that he meant every year, with two horses!

3
Olympic Silver

THAT SUMMER OF 1984 was yet another major turning point in Ian's hectic career with horses, and just as importantly, our own life-style. It was the real beginning of incessant travelling up and down the British Isles. The M6 was becoming a weekly treadmill. No one could understand why we lived in Scotland or indeed why we chose to continue doing so. It was the year of the Olympics but, in many ways more vital for us, it was the year Ian became sponsored. A Scottish-based firm took us over. I had desperately hoped this could happen and we breathed a sigh of relief as soon as the Edinburgh Woollen Mill, in the shape of David Stevenson, took an interest in us. He agreed to sponsor four horses with Ian and was keen to buy more young horses to run in his firm's name. It seemed like a dream and I for one could have cried with relief because the pressure of my coping with the bank manager was becoming a well-known, standing joke in our house! Whenever Ian sent me in to see him about our red accounts he used to say, 'Well, Mrs Stark, what bright ideas have you got for me today?' For once, I genuinely had one, and it was concrete.

Preparation for the Olympics took off with great gusto. Up until then Ian's main dressage help had come from Mrs Barbara Slane-Fleming who is a successful dressage trainer with a wealth of experience. Mrs Slane-Fleming has always taken a great interest in Ian and his horses and has been a terrific help over the years. Now he was to take his horses down to Wylye in Wiltshire, the home of the Hugh Russells. At Wylye other trainers like top dressage rider

Ferdi Eilberg and Pat Burgess, to name only two, were available for coaching the British Team members if they wished to use the instruction. Pat Burgess coaches the show jumping side and has been an incredible help to Ian. She is also a faith healer and helped Ian when he had severe back trouble. Lady Hugh Russell used to compete until she had a hunting accident which left her paralysed. Since then she has become a familiar sight driving her specially adapted Mini Moke at events all over the country.

Lady Hugh gave them all invaluable help with their cross-country training and indeed was a source of inspiration to anyone who had the good fortune to stay there. Her constant energy, enthusiasm and organising ability far outweighed the fact that she was at first a little intimidating! Ian got on well with her and has tremendous admiration for the help he has received from her at Wylye. They must be good friends because he once took Haggis our black and tan terrier puppy to stay there and it pee'd on the carpet right in front of her wheelchair – she just roared with laughter! When accidently he broke a three-hundred-year old pane of glass in the dining room window, I thought he would be automatically expelled from Wylye. He set the burglar alarm off early one morning and once was so late for one of Lady Hugh's organised press lunches that I didn't think he would be allowed back there. When he told me of these incidents I presumed he must be needing help for his nerves, it was so unlike him.

In the build up to the Olympics, many firms presented the riders with gifts of clothes or equipment which they would be able to use out in Los Angeles. I went down to visit Ian at Wylye and to see how the training was going. Everyone was caught up in a hilarious photo-session. As far as I could see they were sponsored with everything except underwear and all the riders were struggling in and out of breeches and boots, puffa jackets, hats which didn't fit etc. The lightweight clothes turned out to be of vital importance because it was so hot in LA you could have died of heatstroke. Both riders and horses needed electrolytes in their diets, so much salt was lost in sweat.

Before leaving for the United States, one of the jaunts Ian enjoyed most was a helicopter ride. Raymond Brooks-Ward, the

Arriving at Santa Anita racecourse, site of the Los Angeles Olympics – Claire Davies with Wattie and Ian with Oxford Blue.

television commentator, had arranged for some of the riders to be uplifted from Wylye and flown to Birmingham for a 'ride and drive' competition at the Royal International Horse Show. It was televised and we were all disappointed at home that Ian didn't win a car to bring back to us. It was amazing that he won anything though, as due to some mix-up they didn't get supper and the sum total of their diet that evening was champagne. Ian and David Green had been scaling up lampposts in an attempt to out do one another. They had been at a reception with Princess Anne so I hope she didn't look out of a window and see them.

Perhaps their high spirits prevailed through the extra long flight ahead of them, out to America. It was a worry for horse-owners and riders alike. It is always a worry sending horses by air. The grooms travel with the horses and must of course be very responsible. The 'plane to America was fully loaded and the horses got very hot and had to be hosed down. It was the first time our horses had been transported by air and to see our two best horses being loaded was very nerve-racking. When they arrived out in LA the team mounts were generally in fairly good shape considering the number of hours they had been airborne, but obviously they were very tired like the riders themselves. It's not surprising that the horses and their grooms did show some symptoms of jet lag as their 'plane's flight was delayed, taken on a detour to refuel, and the flight was much longer than the expected eighteen hours. The riders followed out soon after their horses and needed a couple of days to rest and catch up on their sleep routines. The only horse who never properly shook off jet lag was Robert Lemieux's Gamesmaster who remained seedy for over a week.

Heather Holgate, Ginny's mum, had very cleverly managed to rent a house for the riders' use during their stay for the Olympics. Also staying in the house was our chef d'équipe, Major Malcolm Wallace. This popular and much appreciated member of the team is a former commanding officer of the King's Troop Royal Horse Artillery and has been a successful competitor. To be chef d'équipe is not an easy job: he has to liaise with everyone, make arrangements for the team members and is responsible for all aspects of team welfare. The village provided for the other athletes was rather far away from the Santa Anita racecourse stadium where the dressage and show-jumping were to take place. It was far more pleasant for the British event team to stay five minutes drive away from their horses and have the endless use of a private swimming pool to cool off in. Ian rang me from LA. He said that it was 5.30am and he had just been swimming, first morning there. When he told me the time of day with him I wondered if this trip was going to change his daily routine. He is well-known for being a late riser at home! Since then he's done a few after-dinner talks, mentioning his early morning swim with Lucinda – I don't know who was more taken by surprise when Ian dived in beside her and she was topless!

Dressage day was fast approaching. The team had been finalised as Ginny Holgate on Priceless, Tiny Clapham on Windjammer,

Ian on Oxford Blue jumping through the spectacular 'Ghost Town' complex, Olympics 1984.

Ian on Robbie and Lucinda Green on Regal Realm. The heat was intense. Ginny and Tiny were drawn to go early in the day but even so the temperatures were unbearably high for riding. Team spirit was terrific and they all got on well, keeping each others' morale up in the face of riding under pressure. The climate and the crowds were enough to give even the most experienced competitor stage-fright. In Tiny's case particularly it was nerve-racking. Whilst she was riding around the arena the commentator announced the previous rider's dressage score. It was the American girl, Karen Stive's mark and the home crowd went wild, cheering, yelling and clapping. Windjammer is excitable at the best of times and Tiny did well to get his concentration back at all. Ian later watched on video his test on Robbie. The excitement of just being there, representing his country in that stadium is all rather a blur. As we

47

helped him to peel off a shirt soaked in sweat he couldn't remember any movements of the test he had just ridden. How he didn't lose his way I'll never know. Robbie tried really hard and we were very pleased when he finished on the same mark as Ginny on Priceless. Lucinda was last but certainly not least to go. Her performance was as usual, absolutely polished. Her cool showed no signs of being ruffled even riding in the 'nineties' of the LA afternoon.

The cross-country was some distance away from the city, further south and near the coast. Everything was expected to be a little cooler there, fanned by a breeze from the sea but still excrutiatingly hot, as it turned out, for cross-country riding. The whole camp of horses, riders, grooms and supporters made a general exodus to the Fairbanks ranch for this phase. I felt sorry for Sue, Robert Lemieux's groom left behind to look after the reserve horses, Sir Wattie, Shannagh, Night Cap, and Gamesmaster. Rob himself was a great sport, actively helping everyone else and yet he must have been bitterly disappointed at not riding too.

A new camp established, the cross-country day began. I had travelled out to see the event with one of Wattie's owners, Dame Jean Maxwell-Scott. It was a real privilege to be in her company and what a good owner she is, travelling all that way and knowing that she probably would not even see her horse compete as he was a reserve. Throughout all the baking temperatures she always remained looking immaculate with never a hair out of place, her sun hat fixed on firmly whilst everyone else was melting. Many remarked in admiration at my tall, distinguished companion. We arrived in busloads out at the course early in the morning with hundreds of other spectators. We were walking round it before the riders were even out of their beds in the stable area!

To an enthusiastic crowd, Ginny was first of the British to go. Her neat, competent round with Priceless made the enormous fences look easy, thrilled the spectators and raised the morale of her team-mates. Tiny, as most of us know, came down in the most tricky water combination. Soaked to the skin, she continued on a very difficult round, dogged by bad luck and probably worried that she had let her team down. Frightened that he would do the same, Ian set off. Robbie took the second fence on the cross-country hard with his knees but luckily, somehow he didn't fall. The worst thing was that Ian lost his whip! If anything this mistake wakened the horse up and he was paying attention for the rest of the round.

Lucinda rode in her usual, positive, attacking style. Regal Realm seemed to pull out all the stops and gave that enormous course everything he had, oppressive heat and all. The team soon packed up to return to Santa Anita racecourse for that crucial final phase. In second place, in hot pursuit of their hosts, the Americans, our team kept their fingers crossed that the heat hadn't taken too much out of the British horses.

Ted Edgar stepped in to supervise the practice jump outside the show-jumping arena, probably for Ian's benefit. He gave the team a lecture before they started working in, on the principle that event riders cannot show jump to save themselves. Ian was nearly sick with nerves. It would not have amused him to know that a newspaper reporter phoned Liz Davidson, in Aberdeen, at that very moment, and asked her what it was like to be the owner of a horse, well known to be a useless show jumper! Her jaw just dropped. Her comment must have been unrepeatable never mind unprintable.

The heat was shimmering as each one's turn came. The girls all jumped clear rounds but Ian's performance had us all on the edges of our seats. Robbie was very, very tired. After leaping over an enormous practice jump to try and give him confidence, his strength was oozing away like petrol draining from a tank. He had no energy or enthusiasm left for Ian to call upon. One paper said that Ian's disappointing round lost the gold medal for the British team. I felt that if my husband hadn't been such a strong rider they would have lost the silver as well. There is an expression – 'flogging a dead horse' – and in this case Ian felt he nearly had to carry Robbie round. The horse's feet gently stroked almost every pole and it was probably the worst show jumping phase Ian has ever had to ride.

The final presentation of awards, rosettes and medals was very moving. As a supporter in the stands it was one I'll always remember. First hand experience of Olympics is one not to be forgotten in a hurry. Security is such that you see little of the riders

OLYMPICS 198[

LEFT Relief of tensio[
after the cross-count[
The Brits in team sh[
(*left to right*) Tiny
Clapham, Lucinda
Green, Ian and Ginn[
Leng (then Holgate).

BELOW Oxford Blue
working in well for t[
show jumping phase
only to tire during hi[
round.

OPPOSITE ABOVE Four
very happy riders – la[
of honour time.

OPPOSITE BELOW A pr[
moment, but can't qu[
take it in. Olympics
prizegiving 1984.

and even less of the horses. I usually give Ian any help I can at events such as holding horses or tack and being of assistance in any practical way is normally the way we operate. Owners or their representatives were allowed into the stable area for one hour every day, at midday, and no other time. To get into celebrations, drinking sessions and water fights afterwards was I suppose, some small concession but if I had had the misfortune to be the owner of a sick or badly damaged horse after cross country I would have been irate with frustration and worry. When the competition was finished the supporters travelled home. I could have stayed on to go to Disney World, see some of the other athletic events and watch the Closing Ceremony but my heart just wasn't in it. Participants in the Olympics are of course totally involved in the Games and find it very moving but for those of us on the fringe it is a rather restricted area.

Glad of Dame Jean's company, I flew back with her from Los Angeles. Our home village of Ashkirk was more than keen to give Ian a hero's welcome on his return but he and the horses were not due back for at least another week. This gave us time to get things organised. A party was arranged in Ashkirk Hall but somehow it was going to be a surprise! I couldn't be absolutely certain of the time of Ian's return flight so was worried that a couple of hundred people might be kept waiting. The best plan then was to meet him in London to make sure he boarded without delay a shuttle flight up to Edinburgh. To make an afternoon of it, Jean Slater (a long-standing friend), the children and I, and Granny Stark (who'd never flown before) boarded a plane at Turnhouse Airport to be part of the reception squad in London. Granny was beside herself with excitement and took to flying like a duck to water. We pushed and shoved through crowds to surprise Ian, who couldn't believe his mother had really done the flight. I tried to ignore Stephanie, always prone to asthmatic attacks, who was showing the usual warning signs of over-excitement.

One snag which I hadn't bargained for was yet another press conference in London before we could escape. The minutes were ticking past like seconds and somehow we had to get Ian on the 3 o'clock flight without him being suspicious. The press meeting

A special way to remember the 1984 Olympics. Local enthusiast Pat Whitehead presented Ian with a painting by the late Leesa Sandys-Lumsdaine, from friends in Ashkirk and the Borders.

seemed to take forever. I knew we could only be there another ten minutes at the most. Quickly I had a word in Malcolm Wallace's ear. We shoe-horned Ian, who was protesting vehemently out. 'What's the hurry, there's no rush is there?' Catching the shuttle by the skin of our teeth Ian's attention was then taken up by air hostesses and passengers alike, looking at his silver medal. I don't even know how the kids kept the oncoming party a secret.

Usually the last passenger to disembark, I was first off in Edinburgh and ran like a hare for the car. Ian was laden down with bottles of booze given to him at the Heathrow reception and his pockets were full of miniatures given to him by the stewardesses on the 'plane. Somehow we got everything and everyone shovelled into the car but I was to drive because Ian was so exhausted. He hadn't slept since the Closing Ceremony of the Games and was very jet-lagged, grumbling a lot as I raced down the A7, a twisty road at the best of times. It's not a habit of mine to jump red lights and overtake a lot of other traffic but I was, as they say, very late for a very important date. We rounded the last corner towards home with Ian muttering something to the effect that I should never have passed my test. I airily waffled on about just going to collect the milk in the village shop at Ashkirk and drove him right into the middle of the most spontaneous reception he has ever had.

He got out of the car and stood there in total disbelief. That is one stunt I could never pull again. Ashkirk's cheering crowd gave him a warm welcome back. It was a moving scene and almost too much for Ian, he was so shattered anyway. After the speeches and celebrations were over we drove home to Haughhead to find the house and stables decorated with balloons and streamers. Perhaps the nicest touch of all was that we got the horses up from the south of England in time to share the festivities, thanks to Les Smith driving our lorry hundreds of miles to collect them. Someone said to Ian, 'It's good to see your horses back too,' to which he replied, 'Well, that's funny, I'm not expecting to see them for at least a couple of days!'

After all the excitement was over Stephanie went into hospital the following afternoon, wheezing like a set of bagpipes. This has happened quite a few times now and the more hectic our lifestyle is, the more difficult it is for her to cope with her asthma. It brings us all back to earth abruptly.

4
Burghley 1985

WE SAT SOMEWHAT GLUMLY in Peel Hospital next morning and gave all Stephanie's medical details to the nurses who were trying to cope with her. We both felt totally deflated after all the travelling and celebrations, as we watched her gasping for air and moving restlessly around inside the oxygen tent. It was only when one of the doctors came round the ward that some humour returned on the scene. He said to Stephanie, 'Oh! your Daddy is thingymajig. They've just been out whereveritis. They got a gold medal, didn't they?' he beamed, quite pleased with himself at being so up to date with local news. 'A show-jumper,' he nodded emphatically as he left ten minutes later. Ian shook his head and smiled. We took the medal out of my handbag and it was still silver. It hadn't changed colour overnight in spite of what the doctor thought!

Funny little incidents like that are the ones you remember and also those that keep your feet firmly on the ground. Just as we may have been in the clouds with Olympic success, being on the crest of a wave doesn't last long. At that time, still carried along from Los Angeles, we were quite determined that Wattie would run at Burghley that autumn. With the benefit of hindsight it was a mistake.

Even though he had not competed over there, the trip to Los Angeles and back as reserve horse had completely taken the edge off Wattie. He was well in himself but totally flat and lacking sparkle. Ginny Holgate was riding Night Cap who was also a

55

reserve horse, but being older and more experienced he seemed to have coped with the long trip better than Wattie.

While out on the cross-country at Burghley it was one of those unfortunate occasions when Ian heard the commentary on his round. It sounded good and in his excitement he made a rare mistake of changing his plans for his route through a double bullfinch near the end of the course. Two from home, Ian knew if he could ride them straight that he would move into second place. He was forgetting that Wattie's pet hate is to brush through this kind of fence. He did an enormous leap over the first part and 'was sick' into the second, stopping hard up against it with his near fore stuck in the brush frame. He bruised his tendon sheath as a result, was spun at the Sunday vetting due to slight unsoundness and was then rested for about a year. It was desperately disappointing but a long rest is an absolute must for this sort of injury and he came back the better for time off.

At Wylye three-day event that same autumn a young horse called Ben Rinnes who was jointly owned by Pollyann Lochore and Ian gave himself an injury and Ian couldn't put him forward for the Sunday morning vetting. He tried to convince himself that it was only a deep overreach which was making Rinnes lame and that it would soon mend, but gradually time told us otherwise. He too needed a long time out.

By now our yard was growing and we had put up more stables. Amongst the good young hopes we had coming up were Deansland and Lairdstown and we still had the consistently good Charlie Brown IV.

The hectic 1984 season at last came to a close culminating in Ian winning the British points championship. In many ways, to me, this was the most important trophy which he won that year. It represented all those events which we had been at and all the work that had gone into those summer months. Finally, as a result of taking part in the Olympics, Ian was asked out to New Zealand with some others, as a guest to compete at Pukekohe Horse Trials. He enjoyed this immensely, reliving some Olympic euphoria and having a great holiday at the same time. His hosts out there were extremely kind and their easy-going New Zealand outlook on life

Jenny on Mrs Ann Wilson's brilliant Connemara stallion Smokey Shane. Greenhill, Selkirk 1985.

was a welcome break from home, where there is now always pressure and buzz. People may envy us but I wonder if they would really want the strain of it all.

The excitement of Ian's trip to Los Angeles lasted for weeks, maybe months and didn't settle down. Finally we took the kids away to Austria on a skiing holiday over Christmas and New Year just to get away from everything. Not having been abroad at this time of year before, we hadn't realised just how much stuff we would have to pack up to take with us, Santa Claus going too, but it was so worth it. Anyone with animals knows how important it is just to have a clean break sometimes, especially from horses and their seven day a week demands. We came back refreshed and ready to begin the 1985 season – the year of the European Championships at Burghley.

With Wattie still resting, Ian kept his fingers crossed that Robbie might be chosen for the team there. Our horses began their walking and slow work while the spring entries were soon put in the post, including those special Badminton ones.

Sadly though, the previous autumn's bad luck was not to be shaken off that easily and Ian was heading for a disappointing Badminton. Being very ill before the event he probably shouldn't have even ridden there, but try telling that to someone who constantly suffers from eventing fever anyway. He roared out of the yard in the lorry with Robbie and Lairdstown, his prospective rides that year. Both children and I had caught Ian's flu bug by this time and we were lying in a row in our bed, coughing and sneezing in chorus. The most we were going to see of the great, legendary event was on television. Ian 'phoned us a few times and things didn't sound marvellous at his end. With a raging temperature, I was only dimly aware of friends and neighbours who came to visit, climbing over spare furniture, through plaster dust and all that goes with house alterations. Haughhead and its occupants were certainly in bad shape and when I did switch the television on, it was snowing at Badminton so I presumed that Ian and the two horses were not in great form either! With Lairdstown, a bit of a gamble to take there anyway, he was eliminated very near the end of his cross-country and Robbie had a fall going into the Quarry. Ian was rather depressed when he got home; the final straw had been the horsebox breaking down on the return journey.

Ian was sure that his chances were dashed for a coveted place on the European team in the autumn. When the long list came out with his name on it he felt much better but worried that all his eggs were in the one basket, namely Robbie.

Once Badminton was past Oxford Blue was sent home to Aberdeen to rest. Ian then turned his concentration to Deansland who was entered for Bramham three-day event at the end of May. His whole spring season of competition was nearly over and he hoped for any win that would turn his luck again. Like a gambler waiting for a certain card to appear in his hand, he set off to Yorkshire with Deanie. Thrilled to bits, the win did come and his good fortune returned. This big chestnut horse had completed

Deansland in the wet at Gatcombe 1985.

Bramham twice before with Mrs Ann Short, his owner, and we all knew that the course suited him. Coupled with this, the girl riding VSOP who was lying in the lead on the final day, unbelievably took the wrong course in the show-jumping. It was definitely not the most pleasant note to win on, but a win nevertheless, which gained Deansland a place on the long list for the European Championships. Ian began his autumn programme feeling more confident, with two possibilities for Burghley, or so he thought.

The various build up competitions, team training sessions and final trial at Locko Park were to change all this. British team selectors watch all their potential candidates on these occasions and miss nothing. This event was no exception. As horses came off their cross-country phase at Locko, Peter Scott-Dunn, the team vet, checked their legs, heart and wind. Deansland was roaring like a steam engine and Peter shook his head as he looked over his specs at Ian. He promptly burst out laughing and said, 'You don't really have to say anything, Peter, there's nothing wrong with my hearing!' The horse was duly and successfully hobdayed and given a long rest.

The pace hotted up as the European Championships at Burghley drew nearer. The team was announced as Lucinda on Regal Realm, Ginny on Priceless, Ian on Robbie and Rodney Powell on Pomeroy. The individuals were to be Lorna Clarke on Myross and Clarissa Strachan on Delphy Dazzle. Madelaine Gurdon was named as reserve on The Done Thing but she eventually ran as an individual when Lorna took over Rodney's team place. Pomeroy was unfortunately out of things due to a slight unsoundness, something we all dread our horses having.

After the previous year at Burghley with everything seeming to go wrong when he ran Wattie, Ian was superstitious about his 1985 attempt. If a rider is unlucky a few times at a particular competition it tends to become jinxed for them and Ian was panicking that Burghley was going to be just that kind of unlucky track for him. His fears however were unfounded and the dressage stage passed fairly quietly and Robbie produced his usual, reliable, 'clockwork-mouse' test. In fact it contributed to his lying second overall after cross-country day. Most of the riders were absolutely dreading a horrific looking bullfinch at fence four but on the whole it jumped quite well. There were one or two spectacular spills at it though, not least David Green's very reluctant dismount into the yawning ditch in front of the brush. Many competitors opted for an easier alternative route and as it turned out Ian was sent this way, following team instructions. Lorna gave the crowd their money's worth when she skimmed gracefully through the water jump, seemingly oblivious to another rider still in there! He probably blinked and missed her anyway.

Ian was white as a sheet on show-jumping morning. He would like to have hung on to his second place more than anything but the dreaded phase did it again. One fence down brought him back to third individual place – still something of which he could be very proud. Ginny and Lorna were in first and second places respectively.

The medals were no sooner handed out, the celebrations hardly over when the talk started buzzing about the Australian trip in the spring ahead. The World Championships in Gawler 1986 were now the main event on the horizon. We drew in our horns once more, returned to Scotland, and waited. The long list came out with Robbie's name on it. We wondered if we could dare put the pressure on him yet again. For the lightweight animal which he is, looking nothing like a conventional event horse should, he has given his heart out for us many times. In the following spring he would only be ten but having started three-day events as a seven-year-old and completed six of them, hardly ever out of the money, he had a lot of miles on his clock. If the horse had had a choice in life he would have been a lady's lightweight hunter or point-to-pointer but not a globe trotting three-day event horse. Having won Ian a medal of each colour we decided then that if he went to Australia and no matter what happened there, we would retire him afterwards. In no way did we want him subjected to the rigours of the sport endlessly until he became unsound. A ten-year-old may be young to retire from competition work but a lot depends on each horse's individual outlook. His temperament is not what you would describe as that of a competition horse. Always a gentleman, he is quite happy teaching beginners to ride but out hunting with the Duke of Buccleuch's hounds he can terrify Mrs Stark with his top gear in two seconds flat!

Our last big event for the autumn of 1985 was to be Chatsworth. Ian had just been on a disappointing trip to the Osberton three-day event with a horse called Good News belonging to Edward Pybus. Ian fell off near the end of the cross-country and really put the icing on the cake when he lost his way in the show-jumping and nearly got eliminated. He hoped his trip to the event in the beautiful setting of Chatsworth promised him more luck. Riding his young favourite Glenburnie and Charlie Brown IV Ian set off to try and gain some success from these two. Here I should like to say something about Glenburnie – one of Ian's favourite horses. Originally bred to race, Glenburnie was broken and hunted by Rosi Maitland-Carew. Thinking that his manners needed some improving, the family sent Glenburnie to us as a four-year-old

The children take up riding (*left to right*) Tim on Queenie, Granny Stark, Stephanie on Sugar and Jenny.

while they were away on holiday. On their return Ian suggested that the horse's talent might take him further than the hunting field and said he would love to ride him in a novice one-day event. Nine months later Glenburnie was the Scottish Novice Champion, winning at Thirlestane Castle horse trials.

I was supposed to be at Chatsworth to help but it didn't make things any easier when I went off to deliver a horse to someone, whilst on my way. Having no idea of distance or direction my good intentions took me a few hundred miles and several hours off course. I had a puncture to cope with as well and was having forty fits in case the horse I was delivering to its new home got out of its trailer on the motorway. Meanwhile Ian was sitting stewing, wondering where on earth I was. Nowadays we could keep in touch by carphone but at that time we weren't half so smart. I did eventually pant into Chatsworth as Ian was riding into the start of phase A on Charlie. Some people would have put my arrival down to absolutely perfect timing but Ian gave me rather a filthy look! It was almost as bad as the mud and torrential rain which followed on the Sunday. Glen had gone well in his cross-country apart from a green stop as he came out of the water at the fence called Queen Mary's Bower. He finished twelfth. Charlie was in good form but being a lightweight little horse he could hardly jump out of the deep going in the show-jumping arena and finished ninth.

Ian had had a year of being away from home a lot so we rashly booked ourselves in for a family holiday for a week in the Seychelles. Seven days with no horses to feed or muck out, and time to spend with the kids is a fantastic change. We all got acutely sunburnt and had great fun – but a week was more than enough for Ian. Boredom was setting in. He was quite rightly fed up with jumping off the swimming pool's diving board a hundred times a morning with Stephanie. The main reason for going to the Seychelles in the first place had been the attraction of water skiing but much to all our friends' amusement we picked the one week in the year when the waves were too high for it! We had rounded off the year with a holiday in the sun but Ian was itching to get home, get Christmas and New Year past and start 1986 with a vengeance. With a good string of horses to look forward to working, he was impatient to start and felt very positive about the year ahead. We had a feeling that 1986 was going to be a special year for us but it was hard to explain why. Even the children both being at school now gave me far more time to help Ian work the horses. My favourite pastime is Wattie's slow fittening, so I turned my attention to this quite happily, never guessing how important that was going to be.

5
Wattie's Year

WE DIDN'T REALISE at the beginning of 1986 that during the year we would be travelling all over the world. Ian rode at a total of eight three-day events, five of them abroad, and finished off his season by being invited out to ride and teach in Jamaica. We kicked off preparing for the two major features, Badminton, hotly followed by Gawler, home of the World Championships. Both rather daunting tasks, we were extremely fortunate in having not only the good horses to prepare for these trips but also the excellent help of Iain Couttie working for us. On the brink of going off to set up his own yard and business with horses, he very gladly agreed to look after Robbie for the Australian stint. It was one which required a tremendous amount of organising on every level because if it was to go ahead, it meant nearly six weeks 'down under', two of those in the restrictions of quarantine. We needed someone as experienced as Couttie to deal with as many of Robbie's arrangements as possible because first and foremost the other Ian was full steam ahead for Badminton with two horses, Sir Wattie and Glenburnie.

After Burghley 1984 Wattie had had nearly a year off. We started him again slowly in October 1985. Having been a tiresome youngster in the very beginning we had wondered if he would ever settle to hunting but decided to give it a try to see if his leg was completely better and ready to take the strain of preparing for a three-day event all over again. I hunted him a few times and he was very gentlemanly which surprised Ian because he always thought of him as quite a thug! I reported back one day that he would even

64

Sir Wattie in his winter woollies at Abbotsford with his friend Bunny the donkey and his joint owner Dame Jean Maxwell-Scott.

stand patiently in a queue for a hunt jump whereupon I was blasted by the boss, irate that I should do such a thing anyway! Perhaps it's not surprising though that Wattie enjoyed his hunting, being bred from a mare who was a brilliant hunter and who went out three days a fortnight for seven seasons before being bred off. It was a great success anyway as Christmas saw him cheerful, very fit and his legs looked ready for lots of work. All that January we did slow canter work in deep snow, perhaps the ideal preparation for the bottomless mud he was about to meet in the spring.

Our Scottish weather sees a lot of events cancelled at this time of year, so Ian moved south for a while with a lorry load of horses to use the English circuit of competitions. He took Wattie, Robbie, Glenburnie, Deansland, Kingarth and Yair, a comparative youngster, with him. Most of them were stabled at Mark Todd's yard at Cholderton in Wiltshire while Robbie was at Wylye for team training sessions to prepare for Gawler. Ian was away for many weeks and had Couttie to help him, thank goodness. Anne Cranston and I drove down for a couple of weekends, mainly to see how Kingarth was coming on. He was new to Ian's string of horses and had previously been ridden successfully by Anne in novice and intermediate classes.

We took the kids down with us to Belton Park so that in between classes Ian had to take them to the fantastic adventure playground – an absolute heaven for small children and energetic adults. Ian played Tarzan quite happily in his breeches and boots before the show-jumping phase. The other event I remember vividly is Brigstock when Anne and I nearly turned back on the M6, the driving snow was so thick and horizontal, we thought the event would certainly be cancelled. It wasn't and Ian said jokingly that the weather might have the same idea in mind for Badminton! He is consistently undeterred by deep mud and heavy rain himself. He never expects his horses to worry about such conditions so perhaps that's why they don't. Badminton '86 was to test this theory to the extreme.

At last we reached the important week. It was hard to take it in that not only had it come round again so soon, but the following week we were to be Australia bound. Well, one thing at a time. Iain Couttie dealt with Robbie who was now in strict quarantine at Wylye. The two girls who have helped us a lot, Claire Davies and Sandra Miller took charge of our stable chores at Badminton. The kids were determined to come with me that year, so Sandra and I took them down with us in the train from Carlisle. By the time we had reached Birmingham Stephanie had us red-necked with embarrassment and the whole carriage seemed to know who we were and where we were going. I was glad when the time came to get off. Unfortunately I'd said to Ian to meet us at Cheltenham station and if I had only looked at a map we could have got a lot closer to things and saved him a ridiculous drive to collect us. It was pouring down and hailstones were bouncing off the parked cars at the station. When Ian arrived to pick us up he was quite relaxed about the event, presuming it was all going to be off anyway due to the weather. I was relieved that he was feeling so cheerful as I was expecting a lecture, in the form of a geography lesson, but told myself that perhaps absence does make the heart grow fonder, he seemed pleased to see us all.

The cocktail party that evening also had a relaxed, 'this is not about to happen' feeling and everyone chatted away trying to ignore the splashing of puddles outside. The second day of dressage, Friday, arrived and the torrents of rain seemed to take a pull and ease off considerably. Glenburnie had done a very promising test on the first day and given Ian a great morale boost before he began riding-in Wattie. Ian was last to go into the dressage arena and the mud was at its squelchiest and stickiest. Wattie seemed unperturbed and looked a picture. I hadn't seen him for a few weeks and now he looked toned up and attentive, well aware of where he was and what he had to do. He has always been a horse who remembers surroundings and events from previous years and he certainly recognises Badminton.

After the dressage Wattie was lying in third place and Glenburnie in tenth. The rain started to lash down threateningly and Ian was faced with the big decision of running or withdrawing his horses. Having competed there before, and not seeming to worry about the going, Wattie seemed the obvious choice to run. Glenburnie on the other hand was lacking in experience and could possibly have had a fright on the cross-country in view of the conditions. Ian thought this over and, perhaps opting to save him for another year, withdrew him – quickly, before he changed his mind!

Cross-country day arrived. I don't usually worry unduly when Ian is riding but that year I felt very nervous on his behalf and stayed in the lorry a lot of the time! His third attempt riding there, Ian hoped it might be third time lucky but he had to wait until the very end of the day to find out. When we went up to the start box the rain was just beginning again. It was such dreadful weather that people were starting to go home.

The kids put on their new, white, dazzling Edinburgh Woollen Mill sweat shirts. Effective for the cameras maybe, these were somewhat inappropriate for the weather and absolutely black with mud in no time. Neither of them was the slightest bit worried and I suppose good or bad publicity achieves the same result – I just needed shares in a washing powder firm to cope with the mess. The crowds were definitely thinning out at the start of phase 'A' so Wattie didn't get too excited. The first three phases seemed to pass in mere seconds. The final stretch lay ahead. Fortunately Sandra took both kids out of the way for a while as pressure was mounting while we checked Wattie over in preparation for the last lap. Everyone seemed to be fussing but trying not to. The strain was terrible and the moment of getting Ian back on board didn't come soon enough. The waiting is more nerve-wracking than the watching. Dame Jean Maxwell-Scott, Mrs Susan Luczyc-Wyhowska and Mrs Barbara Slane-Fleming helped the final tack check and Ian gave Wattie a few canter strides across to the start.

I felt so proud of them just then, watching them go and knowing all the hard work that goes into getting to that cross-country phase. Everyone else rushed to the video tent but I didn't really want to watch at that moment. Ian would go over it all again later, and probably many times, so at that point I concentrated on the commentary. The ooohs and aaahs emerging from the video tent told me what was happening anyway. Fingers crossed in my pockets I could see him negotiate the lake in the distance. Safely through that complex I prayed for the rest of his round. I watched the clock, fairly sure that Wattie was pegging away at those seconds and would come in on time, mud and all. He appeared in the distance and I knew he was tired. I could hardly watch the last fence, but breathed a sigh of relief as he finished. Ian was ecstatic and as he says, came in at the end 'in a heap'. It was rather an incorrect way to pull up, with reins flapping and Ian's arms round his neck, Wattie cantered through the finish, his ears pricked as if looking for another fence. He has the heart of a lion and would probably have kept on going.

The course as usual had caused lots of problems and some horrific falls. Not least of these being Lucinda's spectacular dive into the ditch at the Stockholm fence. Wattie's round left him in the lead. Everyone was rushing up to Ian congratulating him as if he had already won the event while I just hoped everything would

OPPOSITE Cross-country day. Badminton 1986.

68

be all right on the final day. Soon, back in his stable, Wattie was tearing into his haynet cheerfully, not nearly as worried about himself as I was! His legs all bandaged up, he was warm, comfortable and resting. Pretending to be oblivious to everything and everyone he munched his hay.

It seemed no time at all until we all packed into the lorry for the night. I hoped it would be more peaceful than the previous one when Ian, supposedly resting up before his cross-country, had been disturbed by the kids and Haggis. The terrier had done a 'whoopsee' on the children's bunk in the middle of the night, causing them to wake up and start roaring and shouting. I woke up to Ian dancing around in a rage at 4 o'clock in the morning throwing the dog and soiled cushions out of the lorry door. Haggis spent the rest of the night outside in disgrace and the kids were lucky that they weren't banished as well.

Exit Haggis and soiled cushion, 4am the night before cross-country! Badminton 1986.

We decided, as show-jumping day promised to be a long one, that we would all go and have an enormous cooked breakfast in the Badminton kitchens. Ian is hardly ever off his food and obviously thrives on pressure if he could eat on this occasion. Everything went down the hatch as far as I could see. Cereal, followed by bacon, sausage, egg, tomato, mushroom and fried bread – anyone else would have needed medical assistance to get out of the canteen but Ian had obviously bargained on missing lunch just once and ate accordingly.

Now it was time to lead Wattie out and stretch his legs before getting him ready for the final trot-up – the phase which reduces most of the riders to nervous wrecks and worries some of them almost more than riding their show-jumping. It is always a great relief if a horse looks well, trots up sound and only needs five minutes brisk walking on that final day of a three-day event. At Badminton the trot-up is always such an elegant affair taking place in front of the big house and before a very interested, enthusiastic crowd. Claire plaited Wattie up and had him gleaming like a new pin. He looked bright and cheerful and drew himself up a couple of inches for the benefit of the audience. On such occasions he trots out at a spanking pace and this was no exception. Several horses were out of the competition on that Sunday for one reason or another. The organisers decided to push on and start the show-jumping early. Many parts of the beautiful Badminton park were under water and spectators were walking in from miles around, unable to drive in and park their cars, with the mud being so deep in places. People were tramping around, mud clogged to their feet. It was undoubtedly an organiser's nightmare and they wanted to get the competition over and done with. Tradestands were packing up before the show-jumping phase was even under way.

Solemnly Ian got changed into his riding gear, to go over and walk the course. By this time he was white as a sheet and nerves were getting the better of him. This showed by his arriving over at the show-jumping arena two minutes before the first horse was due to go into the ring. Ian was far too late to walk the course calmly and take it in. He had to run round and came back panting to a seat in the stands to watch the first few horses go. After about half an hour he couldn't watch any more. Feeling quite sick by this time we went back across to the stables to get Wattie. Ian thought he'd timed it so that there would just be a few horses to go before him, but he still had time to sit and watch quite a few rounds. This didn't make him feel any better, neither did Badminton steward Charles Stratton trying to organise David Stevenson of Edinburgh Woollen Mill to go into the arena for the prize-giving. Ian thought this was a bit premature considering he hadn't even jumped yet and in his present state of mind could easily lose his way and be eliminated. Wattie always stands over at the knee. On this occasion his big knees were knocking. He was heaped up in rugs, Ian was covered up in a long riding mac and the rain poured down constantly. Ian didn't know if he was shaking with cold, wet or nerves. His stomach was a knot. I was thankful that Wattie wouldn't need much working in. We peeled off the rugs and Ian trotted over to the practice jumps. Everyone else had finished with them by now and the area was like a ploughed field. Wattie cantered round as if he was on a cricket pitch. Rachel Hunt went into the arena for her turn and the heavens just opened. It was hard to believe that there could be any rain left in the sky. As Ian went in to jump it was torrential. He cantered over to salute the Royal Box and remembers that he could hardly see where it was.

Wattie jumped boldly and confidently. Ian couldn't believe he had hit the third fence but must just have tapped it because one end of a pole rested off its cup. Had he realised that had happened he might have tensed and knocked out a few more poles. I was standing biting my fingernails beside Alix Stevenson, who got very excited when she saw a fence go so early on in the round. As Ian flew over the last jump the crowds cheered and he knew he'd achieved that life-long ambition he had held since first seeing Badminton ten years before. Could any other win he ever has now mean quite as much?

The rest of that Sunday was a long celebration. Everyone teased David Stevenson about receiving a trophy from Princess Anne in the prize-giving, but as there was a mix-up she presented it to Ian instead so David just had to stand there smiling, empty handed! We went to the Whitbread stand for drinks and photo sessions.

Ian's greatest moment; receiving the Whitbread Trophy from Princess Anne.

Sadly, somewhere in the enormous crowd we lost our three ladies who had sent Wattie off on his great cross-country round. We owed them lunch at least that day but when we turned round they were gone.

The fun continued later that afternoon with a motorbike race or two in the indoor school at Badminton. There were probably only a handful of campaigners left at the event but they totally ignored the large notice on the door: 'This indoor school must be left tidy – as you find it!'

High after the party in the Support Group tent, Ian proceeded to try and ride 'a wall of death' on the kicking boards in the indoor school. His small cross-country bike kept spluttering and stopping, meanwhile, David Stevenson and Stewart Christie (a

well-known Scottish rider) had such a head-on collision with two other bikes that it's amazing they survived to tell the tale! S R Direct Mail had entertained us all with the best of champagne which fired the party spirit for quite some time. Only when David thought he might have broken the odd rib did things start to cool down. When Brian Higham, the highly-regarded Badminton stable manager, looked in the indoor school next morning and saw bike tracks everywhere he must have wondered if some Hell's Angels had been let loose in there during the night! The final few who crawled out for a meal that evening were not so keen on champagne by this time and some was even left untouched.

We decided to travel home on the Monday, after Ian's lengthy interview with Angela Rippon who was writing a book on Badminton. Too tired to face the long drive anyway, it was only fair to rest Wattie properly before setting off for Scotland. David Stevenson and his wife Alix were absolutely delighted with the way things had gone over the weekend and asked Ian to make sure he stopped in Langholm, their home town and business base, on our way back. We reached there late in the afternoon. David had thrown a celebration party for all his workers in the town. We unloaded Wattie in the main street for anyone who wanted to see him and he even drank some of Ian's champagne for the benefit of the cameras. Glenburnie stood sulking in the lorry and kicked it to bits, making a terrible racket because he wasn't getting attention too. After Ian had been in to the reception he was presented with a handsome set of decanters from The Edinburgh Woollen Mill. Then, he was whisked back down the road to Carlisle to the Border Television studios for a hurried interview about his weekend.

By now the kids were tired and fractious. Once again, luckily for me, friends came to my rescue and removed them from the hub-bub to play at a house in Langholm quietly until the party was over. It was dawning on me that we would get home to unpack and re-pack immediately for the Australian trip. Someone had already taken our horses back to Haughhead for us and eventually we fell into the car and crawled home after them. We left Langholm

OPPOSITE Triumphant in the mud. Badminton 1986.

A different way to travel cross-country for Ian, Stephanie and Tim!

OPPOSITE Celebrations in Langholm on Ian and Wattie's return from winning at Badminton with the Edinburgh Woollen Mill managing director David Stevenson handing out champagne.

amidst many good wishes for the World Championships and the certain knowledge that Ian's sponsors were very pleased with his Badminton success.

A final and most generous gesture was that during the prize giving David had given Ian the Badminton prize money. Usually such cash goes back into an Edinburgh Woollen Mill account for buying young horses. We immediately put it towards building an outdoor school at Haughhead. This is something we have needed for a long time, invaluable for training horses at every age and stage. Many people would have built this before altering their house or stables, but we were only glad that at last we had the chance of such an important asset.

6
Robbie's Finale

WE HAD BARELY forty-eight hours at home. Life suddenly felt like a helter-skelter. Arrangements for the kids were of utmost importance. We were to be away for nearly six weeks and our lifestyle is quite unsettling for them. A team of friends, two grannies and Mrs Mionie Brown were organised to look after everything in our absence. Hardly recovered from a big send-off party at Pinnacle, Ancrum, home of the Bruce family, some of Ian's most generous fans, we set off on Thursday 24 April 1986 at 5 am. I had spent an afternoon catching up on letters, bills and 'phone calls. Clothes literally flung into our cases, we kissed our sleeping children and left, to play out Robbie's swansong in the antipodes. We were both absolutely exhausted.

Yet again, Claire came to our rescue and drove us to the airport while most self respecting folk were still in bed. Little did she know that when she left us at Turnhouse to catch the Edinburgh to London shuttle flight, many British airports were fog bound and we would still be sitting at Edinburgh four hours later. Ian's language was choice. What a way to start our Australian venture. I thought he was really going to strangle the tartan bedecked lady who sold us the tickets. We were meant to be at a champagne reception given by Piper Heidsieck at Gatwick and there was certainly no chance of us getting there. All the others had gathered in London by this time – Virginia Holgate, Lorna Clarke, Clarissa Strachan, Mandy Orchard and Anne-Marie Taylor – and thought that we were still so busy celebrating in Scotland that we hadn't caught our 'plane. If only they had known, Ian was doing a war dance on the airline's reception desk! He glared at me in case I left the luggage and went to tackle someone, anyone he could get hold of, about being palmed off with economy tickets to Hong Kong.

One of the best things about our delay was meeting Mrs Susie Barley. Wife of an air pilot, she is a 'flying mum', quite used to going with unaccompanied children (like us!) as they travel round the world to their parents or schools. She cheerfully whizzes all over the globe like a shuttlecock and very kindly looked after us. Spending a lot of her time at one of her homes in Hong Kong she took us with her so that we could sleep off some jet lag and then she and her husband showed us round lots of the sights of Hong Kong. It was a trip in itself to be remembered but I gather we missed out on an energetic shopping spree which the others had as they passed through. It was so hectic they nearly missed their connecting flight to Melbourne. One of them narrowly squeezed on board as they were closing the doors – weighed down with parcels, I'm told!!

We went to departure lounge thirteen and trying to ignore the superstition, flew on to Australia ourselves. Ian had a broad grin as he was handed tickets to first-class seats. I laughed when he sneezed so hard he blew his earphones off. We watched a film on the rigours of the great Alaskan Husky race, and, another on the Paris to Dakkar car rally. Both seemed to involve the race against time, conditions, discomfort and distance and there were broad similarities to us battling out to Australia for Ian to ride in a three-day event.

It seemed like a week till we arrived in Melbourne. Neither of us ever wanted to see an anaemic looking omelette and sausage ever again. We were sitting sharing the second half of Jilly Cooper's novel *Riders* when a tall chap shot past with a green riding boot bag. It was Mark Todd hurrying to check in for the final stretch to Adelaide. He hadn't bargained on us tagging along but certainly wasn't getting rid of us because he had a lift organised to meet him at the other end – and we hadn't!

We ended up at our quarters in Adelaide which was the Police Training Academy, a grim place for a fortnight. It was no wonder all the students had a habit of saying, 'How are ye?' all the time, just in case you'd died in the last ten minutes. We were keen to get out to Torrens Island where the horses were stabled. Grooms and their charges all looked well and at least there was an area for exercising in quarantine even if it was completely flat and uninspiring – like the sandwiches they provided daily.

The compulsory two weeks passed, greatly helped by skipping, word games, visits to films like *Out of Africa*, (Ian and Toddy fell asleep), *Down and Out in Beverley Hills*, and *Crocodile Dundee*, swimming, water-skiing, water-sliding – anything to pass the time as each rider only had one horse to work and not enough to do! Lord Patrick Beresford had succeeded Malcolm Wallace as chef d'équipe and he must have known that he did not have an easy task ahead of him. A group of people, mostly confined to each other's company for all the weeks involved on this trip, are bound to create an atmosphere, tense at times.

On top of this there were many official functions we all had to attend. There was a very funny side to some of them. At one dinner Lord Patrick fell asleep and Clissy laughed so much I thought she would need to be scraped off the floor. One barbecue in the centre of Adelaide never took place which was strange as there were two thousand people wandering around looking for it in a park. At a reception in the Adelaide Hilton there was a photo session which Ian thought he would brighten up by jumping on to a model horse – the management of the poshest hotel in the city were not amused! We were nearly thrown out. After a wine and cheese evening Ian had to talk his way out of a contretemps with the Adelaide Police. It no doubt helped enormously when he gave his address as the Police Academy at Fort Largs. They just laughed and waved him on.

At another reception a group of us were chatting to Prince Philip. When he realised Lorna was in our midst he said to her, 'But you're not still riding, are you?' and at another someone asked her if she was 'Ginny Holgate's mother?' While the rest of us burst out laughing these remarks went down like a lead balloon. Anyone who had seen her water-skiing expertly on the Murray River wouldn't have had any doubts as to the fact she was 'wee Clarkie'! Mark Todd nearly finished Ian off on this occasion. Turning the speed boat at about 70 mph he spun Ian on the skis, out on a circle, sending him cartwheeling across the top of the water and he thought his end had come. When he finally smacked down Ian wondered if every bone in his body was broken. I was sunbathing on the bank with my eyes shut but I heard the engine roaring and then cut out. There was complete silence and then I heard Ian swear – voices travel clearly across water don't they?

Not all the press were as well informed as they could have been. At the press day one journalist asked Ian which phase he had come over for and when he said all three she looked at him in disbelief!

It was quite a relief to get everyone and the horses moved out to Roseworthy Agricultural College, the base they were to use during the actual competition itself. Having been given the loan of several Rover cars for their stay, the riders could all get around quite a bit to see and do things. Soon all the teams and competitors had arrived and were working their horses together, the sense of competition was stronger. Up until then the American horses had been in quarantine elsewhere and the New Zealand team, apart from Mark Todd and Charisma had not yet come over.

When the other Kiwis arrived everyone felt the event had begun. As a team they were in top form. They all looked bright, cheerful and fit, running everywhere in their black and white track suits. Then, out of the blue disaster struck. One of their horses dropped down dead during canter work. An air of gloom affected everyone. It seemed to be a really bad start to things. By some incredible twist of fate the same thing happened to an Australian horse about a week later and everyone wondered which country was going to be next.

For the first week out at Gawler our team lived in a small private house. This gave us considerable freedom to do as we pleased and cook our own meals, thereby missing out on canteen food which we had largely been living on. The result was that Ginny, Lorna and I pushed our culinary talents to the fore preparing supper for as many as twenty people one evening. It was a great chance to return some of the hospitality we had received. We were able to have four people over from Linsey Park Stud who had looked after the riders and horses so well when we had the fantastic opportunities to go there and use their training facilities. The British team is no doubt indebted to Colin Haynes for allowing them to exercise and gallop at his fabulous stud.

On these occasions the Brits went sightseeing as well – mostly to the famous wineries in the Barossa Valley. Clissy drove us all mad when she came out of a souvenir shop with a toy Koala Bear which played 'Waltzing Matilda' non-stop!

One evening back at the house things were getting a bit strained. The day hadn't gone too well and Ginny had introduced me to someone as Anne-Marie. Supper was supposed to be one of our easier 'cordon-bleu' evenings. It's a standing joke between us that Ginny stood there and solemnly told me in great detail how to cook sausages to make sure they didn't burst. I gritted my teeth and put this down to mounting tension as the competition drew nearer!

We were having the grooms over on another evening and as they were about two hours late we realised they had got lost. Iain Couttie was driving their Land-Rover and he is good at losing his way at the best of times. Realising he had gone wrong he had been driving too fast to make up time. On the way the Land-Rover hit a bump in the road and Chris Hope (Anne-Marie's groom) tried to make a sunroof. Poor Chris staggered in to the house clutching her head and neck, looking concussed. Anne-Marie was absolutely livid and said she was after some part of Iain Couttie's anatomy if he ever drove like that in future! I thought the atmosphere was definitely becoming a bit strained.

We got the chance to see two Australian one-day events just before the Gawler week began. We drove miles and miles to see the first one out at a place called Claire and it took so long to get there that all we saw was the show-jumping. Lots of people seemed pleased that we had made an effort to drive out there though, and we were introduced to 'bundies' which seem to be more rum than anything. At least that's what it felt like on an empty stomach. On the way home we all stopped at a pub and Clissy looked settled in for the evening. As Ian and I were not of the same mood and were ready to leave, we got called 'a couple of boring old farts'!

The other event was at Reynella. Lorna, Clissy and Anne-Marie decided to run their horses there as a warm up for Gawler. The other riders opted to save their rides for the main event not wanting to lame them on the stony going before the big competition. Ginny did the dressage and show-jumping but pulled out of the cross-country. Some of us piled into a car to go out and spectate and support fellow compatriots. Unfortunately, Ian was driving because he always says he is a hopeless passenger. Bill the blacksmith came along because he had heard about Ian's techniques behind the wheel and was keen to get first hand experience. On the way there Ian braked so hard when lights changed that he left skid marks fifty feet long to a screeching of brakes and smell of burning tyres. Bill was impressed, or something. Certainly he looked a bit pale. On the return journey Ian was mucking around with the automatic windows. He succeeded in jamming the switches so that the back windows were stuck open all the way home and the three of us in the back were frozen stiff for two hours. Ian laughed himself sick as we crawled out with our hair windswept and standing straight on end! Bill, for one, won't be in a hurry to be driven by Ian again.

The Gawler week began with Ferdi Eilberg arriving to see how the team's dressage was doing. The riders were driven down to the competition site to view the preparations and stable area to be used during the event. They were soon to be allowed to exercise at Gawler Racecourse itself and use the dressage practice arenas with Ferdi. Although the event was about to start there was still a tremendous amount of work being done at the stadium. It was rather disconcerting that the organisation still had so much to do and so little time to do it in.

To break the monotony for the horses the team travelled them up to the hills behind Gawler on some days, to keep fit and do slow canter work. The hills were incredibly steep and the work for the horses was very strenuous. The riders had a good chance to see the Australian sheep farming methods as in this part there was nothing but sheep for miles around. One of the main problems of the World Championships had been that our horses were extremely fit before they left the UK and the waiting weeks involved, meant maintaining peak fitness without them going 'over the top'.

After we moved into Roseworthy the riders were soon organising their meetings and planning their course walks. The horses were trotted up early every morning under the eagle eye of Peter Scott-Dunn the team vet. The reports were always the same about Robbie. He never could be dragged straight out of his box and look his best. His rider doesn't enjoy being wakened up either!

Without too many hitches dressage day duly arrived. Clissy was first to go on Delphy Dazzle and kept really calm in view of the exciting surroundings of the arena. Mandy came in on Venture Busby, oozing with determination. The horse had been naughty that morning and Mandy was not going to let this happen again in the test. Anne-Marie was next and rode Justin Thyme into the lead after the first day, causing great excitement. Lorna followed and amazingly enough Myross didn't tense and shorten as much as he could have in the electric atmosphere of the stands – he had every excuse with crowds milling around and flags flapping in the wind to distract him.

Team spirit was high and strong. We walked the long, hilly cross-country for the second time en masse. On the way up to Heather Holgate and Dot Willis' house, which overlooked part of the course, we had been hanging out of the Land-Rovers to see half-finished fences but now, it seemed weeks later, we were all studying the finished articles. Photographers and press were on the loose all over the place, grabbing shots of the riders at every obstacle. Cameras clicked and whirred at the water jump while the team waded and mused over all the alternatives and possibilities. We took a wheel with us and checked distances which was probably a waste of time because we didn't have time checks at all the different points each rider wanted checked. I walked part of the way with Ginny's husband Hamish Leng who christened me 'slippers', thinking I was quite nuts, stomping along in a pair of multi-coloured mocassins – I didn't have my green wellies with me and it was raining!

On the second day of dressage the only horse which did an immaculate test was Finvarra with Torrance Fleischman. Ian was disappointed with his effort but at least it didn't pour with rain as it did during some tests, and Robbie didn't explode as many horses had done. The stands were not nearly as packed as those in LA but as the horses moved through from the sand practice arena to the

Victory down under. World Championships, Gawler, Australia 1986. (*Left to right*) Ginny Leng on Priceless, Ian on Oxford Blue, Lorna Clarke on Myross, and Clissy Strachan on Delphy Dazzle.

main ring the atmosphere still made most competitors tense a little. Priceless came in, very 'full of beans' and not needing much of an excuse to misbehave whilst Charisma was also very much on his toes, putting both these top riders under a lot of pressure.

Saturday, May 24 brought cross-country day. The riders had the most unusual maze of roads and tracks and steeplechase to negotiate before going up to the top of a hill for their cross-country. The first roads and tracks went one way round the racecourse and after the steeplechase riders changed the rein and rode several times round the outside of the racecourse again in the opposite direction. It was upsetting for many of the horses as they passed each other and could see one another on the different phases, usually these are well-spaced out from each other.

When Clissy set off on the cross-country itself and had a crashing fall into the water everyone felt demoralised because the water complex was early on in the course. Three of the first four competitors fell at this combination confirming my fears that this fence had a trick element about it, catching out bold horses, making them fall – surely not what the sport is about? Many others fell there, including Mark Todd and Charisma. Ian and Robbie slipped up and parted company on the wood chip surface after a downhill fence. I watched them on the video as Ian swung his legs up round Robbie's neck trying to believe he hadn't really come off! The course caused no end of trouble and a lot has been said about it. Tinks Pottinger did a beautiful round on Volunteer but on the other hand Torrance Fleischman finished on a very tired Finvarra with blood pouring from his nose having hit his face on a fence. What do the public remember most?

The British team went forward to show-jumping Sunday in second place but the vetting that morning was to change around a lot of the results so far. Several horses didn't come forward to be checked and several were spun by the vets, leaving about twenty-five horses in the competition on the final day of the World Championships. It was a disappointingly small number in view of the standard of event and the effort and expenditure involved in getting the whole show on the road.

The Closing Ceremony was a show of mixed feelings. There was great sadness about the New Zealanders' bad luck and Tinks Pottinger having to withdraw Volunteer on the last day. The British team did win the gold, and Ginny and Priceless won a well-earned individual gold but our team couldn't help feeling they had robbed the Kiwis of victory. Perhaps over and above everything was a euphoria that a long spell of training and waiting was finally over. The celebrations were something else and said it all. Ian sat on the 'plane the following morning picking splinters from his hands trying to remember climbing up tent poles the night before!

7
More Travels

WITH A HUGE EFFORT we got up early on that Monday morning
after the World Championships. Struggling with hangovers and
pretty exhausted we fell in and out of cars and aeroplanes as we
made the homeward journey. When an event is over, we are usually
fairly agreed on packing up and clearing out so this is just what we
did – but, it was at a ridiculous hour in the morning. In fact I don't
know why we bothered going to bed at all because we had so much
clobber to stuff into our suitcases and bags.

It was a great relief to get back and see that there hadn't been too
many disasters in our absence. The washing machine went into
overdrive and I wondered if I ever wanted to live out of a suitcase
again. Well, the answer was to be sooner rather than later. We had
less than two weeks until an event at Le Touquet in France. Iain
Couttie got back with Robbie from Australia, had a day off, then
drove out again with Glenburnie to team up with the Holgates for
the French trip.

In the meantime, the two of us tried to sort ourselves out. Often,
Ian gets low after a really big event and this was one of those
occasions. We were in reverse gear as far as getting organised for
Le Touquet was concerned. The horse and groom were there but
we certainly weren't anywhere near leaving. I couldn't get any
sense out of Ian as to how we were going to get across there
ourselves. Various suggestions were vaguely aired but no definite
decisions reached as to flight, ferry, hovercraft, or what it was to
be. Pearl, Ian's mother, was staying for the week we were supposed

to be in France. On the Sunday night when we should at least have been well on our way Ian was lying in a heap in front of the television. 'Taking a grip of myself,' as the saying goes I stomped upstairs and packed the cases. Ian's mum thought I had gone to bed so she nearly had a heart attack when I came back into the sitting-room and said, 'Right, please check that I've got everying in the cases, Ian. If we leave now and drive to Dover we can catch the first ferry in the morning.'

It was midnight when we left and the drive took us less than six hours. We pulled up at Dover at dawn, in time to watch the sunrise. This may sound romantic but things weren't particularly romantic at that moment. I was stuck in the passenger seat under a pile of luggage and coats and felt like something the cat had left behind. Unfolding ourselves from the car, rubbing our eyes and yawning we searched for a coffee bar. There were no queues at that time of day so we soon booked our crossing and the ferry trip went over smoothly while we ate breakfast, like it was going out of style.

Le Touquet was fairly easy to find once we got to the other side of the Channel and as we bombed along twisting country roads I tried not to think about the fact that the car was not insured for driving on the Continent. In fact, Ian himself wasn't insured throughout the whole of that year when he probably did more competing than ever before. It was just one of these things we never got round to doing.

Iain Couttie was pleased and relieved to see us when we arrived but he knows that we are always late for everything so probably wasn't surprised that he was the only groom still waiting for his rider to appear. We spent the most lovely week at this event which had such a relaxed atmosphere. It would be a charming place for a family holiday. The weather was kind to us and lunch was outside under the trees every day. All the supporters got together for this meal, contributing something. We all sat down to fresh bread, pâte, cheese and fruit – and a few bottles of wine as a finishing touch.

The event turned out to suit Glenburnie very well as it was being run at Le Touquet racecourse itself and so the cross-country was comparatively flat. It was only his second three-day event and not as strenuous as many Ian could have chosen. When Ian was actually riding out on the course I could see most of the jumps he was doing from the grandstand. From fence seven onwards his style seemed to change drastically and I couldn't imagine what on earth he was doing. I didn't realise that his stirrup leather had snapped until I was told by a spectator who could see what had happened through his binoculars. Ian was trying frantically to keep in balance and make it through the finish flags. Most of us might have given up in these circumstances with several maximum fences, a Normandy Bank and some sharp drops still to negotiate. Anyone who knows Ian would realise that he would keep going, even if it was only because he was extremely annoyed. Iain Couttie and I could only stand and watch helplessly, knowing that one of us was really going to catch it from Ian in five minutes time. The worst of it was that just before Ian had set off we had been discussing how elderly some of our tack was getting. Fortunately everyone made such a fuss of Ian's ride, and he himself felt that Glenburnie had gone well, that his temper had cooled quite a lot by the time he spoke to us and he was just about able to laugh – even if unable to walk and somewhat bow-legged!

Ginny had also had an exciting round for different reasons. With Murphy going well she went bounding off onto her steeplechase phase only to come upon the previous competitor lying on the ground and a riderless horse cantering about. No one in particular seemed to be in charge of things except for one person vaguely slowing her down to stop. This official obviously didn't speak English (neither did Ginny just then) and so she quickly thought the best thing to do in the circumstances was to gallop back to the start and prevent any more competitors from being released on the course meantime. There was no sign of an ambulance for the body, or anyone standing noting Ginny's time while she was being held up. Blood pressure rose sharply in the Holgate camp while this incident was taking place. We could all see what was happening in the distance but could do nothing to help as the steeplechase section lay on the far side of the racecourse. Heather Holgate was ready to chop up an official for lunch when fortunately someone high up on the organising side came and assured her in broken

English that Ginny would not have time penalties. Thank goodness, we could all breathe again!

It is an event I'll remember because everyone seemed to get on well with one another. We were lucky enough to have a beautiful flat to stay in, near the competition, lent by the Wares family for our use. The two newer members of the squad, Lucy Thompson and Claire Oseman were good fun to be with and I thought very promising riders for teams in the future. Richard Walker, Tiny Clapham and Clissy Strachan also shared this trip, all hardened campaigners! Mary Gordon-Watson, team chef d'équipe, must have been well pleased with the results. A team win and yet another individual win for Ginny, promising a brilliant future for Murphy Himself.

The only sad part which will stick in our minds was the death of a young Polish rider near the end of his cross-country. After the horses had all completed that day, many people put out flowers and wreaths at the jump where he was killed and it served as a reminder that eventing is indeed a high risk sport.

Ian and I set off home on the Sunday night after the show-jumping phase, and most of the celebrations. The other continental competitors were leaving so there would just be a handful of Brits resting up until the next day. Ian was already thinking ahead to his next outing at Luhmühlen in Germany so there seemed no point in us staying on in France. We made good time homewards to start with and caught the last ferry. Unfortunately we hadn't got far from Dover when we were stuck in monumental, motorway traffic jams. After a few hours driving, only covering a few miles, we had to give up and pull into a motel. We woke up at lunchtime the next day! The celebratory French champagne had been more powerful than we thought at the time!

We really had to get back up home though as we had a succession not only of young horses coming in to work for various owners, but also an equal number of young people coming to stay for short training spells. Not least of these to be reckoned with was young Gavin Hennig, all the way from Australia. His father had made the arrangements for his stay with us during an extremely boozy party at the World Championships. Ian couldn't remember much about it but apparently Gavin was coming to live with us for three months and do lots of work on improving his dressage riding. Neither of us had met Gavin before so when his father rang to say he was arriving in Edinburgh airport the following day, Ian made a horrible face at me and I was sent off to collect our Aussie guest. Meeting a zombified stranger off a 'plane is probably not the best time to chat. Gavin was horrified at our Scottish countryside. He found our narrow, twisting roads quite claustrophobic after the open spaces of Australia. He looked in vain for patches of desert. His main topic of conversation was about compact discs. I honestly hadn't a clue what he was saying half the time and he couldn't understand me either. When lingo problems became too much, he would just give up and say 'no worries!'

All in all, Gavin had a tough three months staying with us! We expected him to muck out stables and plait horses which was not second nature to him. He learned a lot and worked hard but it annoyed me intensely to come round the corner and find him standing on top of the muck heap playing an imaginary guitar. To be fair, he had to take most of the work load at the time as Sandra, our full-time help had an extremely nasty fall from Charlie Brown, whilst only out on walking work and broke her pelvis. In return for his training Gavin was to end his stay with us by riding in a couple of novice events, but also he was to be Ian's only groom out at Luhmühlen.

Ian was really looking forward to going out to Germany, and made the excuse that because it was to be the home of the European Championships in 1987, he was keen to see what kind of terrain it was. However, they very nearly didn't go. We have an unspoken rule in our yard that riders out exercising on their own do not lark around and jump fences on my mother's farm. Gavin was only supposed to be walking off Charlie Brown one morning after the horse had just done his last cross-country school before the trip to Germany. We would never have known what Gavin had been up to if he hadn't had to account for a completely smashed up saddle and come in leading the horse home. For some reason, known only to himself he had put Charlie at an unjumpable five-bar gate down a steep hill. The horse had slipped at the last minute, falling over backwards and bursting the gate open. Luckily, neither horse nor rider was hurt. Many people would have put him on the first 'plane home.

Amazingly Charlie showed no signs of loss of confidence. Ian jumped him straight away after the accident and much to our relief, the little horse was going well. The next day Iain Couttie arrived to drive Ian, Gavin and the horse down south to team up with Mark Todd and Lucinda Green to travel out to Luhmühlen.

We had squeezed in a few Scottish events to start our autumn season so I was quite glad to stay at home and give this trip a miss. We had several horses in work which I could keep going in Ian's absence and also we were worried about Glenburnie. Only days before he had pecked badly in the water jump at Eglinton Horse Trials and skinned both his knees. Ian was sure the big grey horse was not going to be right in time for team training for an event in Poland, or the chance of running at Burghley. Having missed Badminton in the spring, Ian did not want to have to withdraw him from this one as well.

With all these thoughts in the back of his mind Ian went off to Luhmühlen, hoping it would be an 'easy' one for Charlie Brown (or CB as we call him). Mr and Mrs Harold Whitson, from whom we lease the horse, went too. The course turned out to be enormous. I didn't know who would be more nervous, Ian, CB, or Mrs Whitson. Ian 'phoned me late each night and said that it was a super event and they were all being well looked after. However he thought that 'the course would terrify the pants off Charlie'. Mrs Whitson gave Ian her usual, morale boosting pep-talk about Charlie being the toughest, soundest horse he will ever ride. At moments like this, I think she forgets that Charlie nearly killed her out hunting by depositing her, breaking some of her ribs and puncturing one of her lungs.

As Toddy, Lucinda and Ian got together and rode as a Commonwealth team, Rowena Whitson had the added bonus of saying that 'her' horse ran in an international three-day event, both as an individual and as a team member, which was a very satisfying result. Anyone who remembers this horse away back in the beginning knows that he was once quite a reluctant jumper. As it turned out he went brilliantly on the Luhmühlen cross-country, respecting the well-built fences. Just as things were going so well and everything was set fair for show-jumping day, we were reminded what great levellers horses are. Our team was in the lead and managed to hold on to this place, in spite of Charlie having a very unexpected fall in the show-jumping arena. Something distracted him, he caught a pole between his front legs and came down on his side, firing Ian into space. He remounted quickly and finished his round with about fifty penalties, not affecting the team position but losing his own place which would have been in the top six competitors.

When he 'phoned home that evening he was a bit fed up but at least had not been hurt and otherwise had had a very good event with Charlie. There were moments when he could have strangled Gavin but that was beside the point. He was due to fly home the next morning to meet up with Iain Couttie who by this time had driven down to Badminton with Glenburnie, Sir Wattie and Kingarth for team training work. Whereas this all used to take place at Wylye in Wiltshire, the sale of that estate necessitated a new venue for team workouts. Badminton turned up as a marvellous alternative, very largely due to the Duke of Beaufort's incredible enthusiasm for the sport. Being fairly central, all the necessary team trainers can get there easily and Frank Weldon and the Willis brothers have built the riders some excellent cross-country schooling fences to use.

The next big event on the horizon for which they were all getting ready was the Open Championships at Gatcombe, home of Princess Anne and Mark Phillips. Ian was due to ride Kingarth in the advanced class and Sir Wattie and Glenburnie, his two prospective autumn team rides, in the championship section. Anne Cranston, the kids and I went down to stay a couple of nights at Badminton, (I don't think we were meant to be there), and went across to Gatcombe each day with Ian, Iain Couttie and Gavin who by this time had got back from Luhmühlen. Anne and I took the chance to ride out Kingarth and Wattie in Badminton Park which was a very memorable morning for us. As we will probably never compete there it is still quite something to say we have ridden

Ian on Jonjo and Stephanie on Foxy at Selkirk Common Riding 1986.

there. It is such a beautiful estate and part of the world I can see why Ian is tempted to move to that area. However . . .

Things were going along smoothly and the kids were having a ball. Charging around on their bikes in Badminton stable yard, they were in their element. I had one rather anxious moment though. One morning the Duke was carefully mounting his frightfully smart horse to go off on a lovely peaceful morning exercise. As he eased himself into the saddle Stephanie said loudly and clearly, 'Hey, you! Why are you not wearing a hat? You'll probably fall off you know!' I nearly died. If only I could have crawled under the paving stones at that moment I would have.

94

Fortunately, he looked mildly amused and telling her she was quite right he rode off.

We went on to Gatcombe Horse Trials that morning. As the day proceeded we made frequent use of the very efficient taxi service, from the lorry park to the show-jumping arena, provided by white Range Rovers. On one such trip the driver took us through the car park. Stephanie misses nothing, 'Was that a dead dog, Mummy?' I tried to ignore this as the heads turned round and eyebrows shot up. 'Mummy is that not Mark Phillips over there?' Before Stephanie persisted with more questions I was very glad our driver accelerated.

Gatcombe was an event of mixed results for Ian. He says himself that he rode the young horse, Kingarth, completely wrongly into the road crossing early on in the course. Coming at it too strongly meant they parted company at the second half of it. We felt it was so disappointing for Anne too. With Glenburnie in the lead after the dressage Ian had to withdraw him from the rest of the event before he was tempted to run him. The horse's knees had not yet fully healed over and Ian still quietly hoped that he would be better for Burghley. He also had our Scottish Championships at Thirlestane strongly in mind, this is our local event and was then just a week away.

This left all eyes on Wattie, still to go. He was lying second to Bruce Davidson and J J Babu, after the dressage and show-jumping. The cross-country ran in reverse order of merit which is unusual thank goodness, and puts far more pressure on the riders. Gatcombe is a hilly course and very testing. Wattie dropped to fourth place after completing it because he simply wasn't ready to go any faster at this stage of his training.

Due to some problems in sorting out Wattie's joint ownership before the autumn season began, the horse had come into work several weeks later than he should have done. We were very relieved when David Stevenson stepped into discussions on our behalf and sorted out the whole thing financially for us. It had been a very worrying time as we thought we were going to lose Wattie from our string of horses if he was put on the open market as had been suggested. Now he is actually jointly owned by David

Stevenson and Dame Jean Maxwell-Scott, although he always competes in the Edinburgh Woollen Mill name under the terms of Ian's sponsorship contract. We will always be grateful to the two Maxwell-Scott sisters and Mrs Luczyc-Wyhowska for their support over the last few years and also for arranging that Wattie always goes back to his home at Abbotsford when he is resting from events.

We are equally indebted to the Maitland-Carew family at Thirlestane Castle, Lauder, Berwickshire, the home of the Scottish Championships. It is also where Glenburnie hails from. Ian often says that this big grey is his greatest hope for the future. At the Thirlestane event of the summer 1986 he was third in the same section as Wattie who won the class. Glenburnie has always been consistently talented and also rather a show off which can be a help when the audience is a panel of dressage judges! His 'see-me' attitude to life gains him popularity with many of Ian's fans who write and ask us for signed photos of Glenburnie.

The fact that Ian's horses all ran well at Thirlestane in 1986 was a big morale boost and was probably in many ways the highlight of our summer. Because it is such a local event Ian was desperate to do well and I have never seen him so nervous as before this event – far more so than before some of the big competitions he has ridden in the south. I was surprised because he is usually unliveable with after a big competition but this was the first time I'd seen him so on edge beforehand. Perhaps it was because he was secretly hoping to pull off the win, which Wattie duly did for him, and it meant such a lot to him. He always admits that he is a very competitive person and that's what I think keeps him going at the level at which he now rides.

8
The Tail End

1986 WENT ON like a whirlwind, spinning us here and there. One moment we were at home and in the next, found ourselves at Burghley with Glenburnie, Ian's favourite. Gavin Hennig, the Australian boy was taken down there as groom. I arrived in the evening after the dressage to be told by him that Ian had nearly been eliminated for missing his test. Apparently he had completely miscalculated his time to start and only left himself a few minutes to canter from his stable to the arena. Someone had rushed forward and hastily grabbed Glen's tail bandage as he was going in to begin. As a result, Mike Tucker, the commentator, teased Ian all weekend about being the most 'laid back' competitor. Several people asked him if he needed a new watch or was he trying to attract additional sponsorship from one of the more famous wristwatch companies? It made things even worse when he got his time totally wrong on cross-country day as well and was almost a minute inside the time. No one would believe that he had made a really genuine mistake but it certainly drew a lot of attention. One or two sharp letters about his ride reached the columns of the horse magazines and believe me they stung for a long time. Perhaps their writers might have held back had they known the agonising decision Ian was going to have to make about a hobday operation for Glen. The horse went on to be fourth and a few days later Ian booked him into the vet's operating theatre. I was at home and he 'phoned me in a state of depression about the whole thing. It seemed such a drastic

Effortless jumping – Glenburnie at Burghley 1986.

decision to take but why wait until the following year? With hindsight, I'm sure we did the right thing.

It seemed no time at all before we were heading out to Poland to run Sir Wattie at Bialy Bor. This three-day event was held miles and miles from anywhere and it seemed to take forever getting there as we travelled across the country by taxis after our flight into Warsaw. It was an incredible experience to visit this beautiful landscape and a lesson to us all. That trip showed us just how much freedom of movement and what a high standard of living we have in the West. My last memory of that country, as we drove along jammed into antiquated minibuses, was of the people working on the land. There were farmers driving horses in carts and ploughs, cows tethered by the roadsides, few tractors to be seen anywhere

A proud chef d'équipe (Lord Patrick Beresford) parades his winning team.
Poland 1986.

and there were lots of old people picking potatoes by hand in the
fields. Considering that rationing of food and petrol is in force out
there, our hosts were very, very kind and looked after us well.

It was beautiful autumn weather throughout our visit and a fun
event for all the riders. Yet again they all got on well with each
other and I don't recall any major hiccups, team rows or blow-ups.
Ginny looked as immaculate as ever on Night Cap, and Rodney
Powell spent a week dieting, or so he said. Anyone who can scoff a
tin of peaches in two seconds like he does, and eat chocolate like it's
going out of style, can give Ian a run for his money in the sweet
tooth stakes. Jane Thelwall had an extremely nasty fall on the
cross-country but fortunately both horse and rider were all right

One way of trying to open a bottle of champagne. Poland 1986.

and continued. Rachel Hunt probably broke the sound barrier on Piglet and Madeleine Gurdon had some difficulty restraining The Done Thing at times. Being a strong-willed little horse he jumped out of the back of the steeplechase start box before getting turned and on his way – in the right direction. On the cross-country itself he decided to run along the bottom of the ditch instead of jumping over it as he was supposed to!

After Ginny's popular win Heather Holgate miraculously produced the food for a tremendous party for everyone who was there to share in their celebrations. We have experienced her excellent and generous hospitality many times and her energy and stamina are to be admired.

We were distinctly lacking in these two qualities as we just managed to fly back home in enough haste to be at the Central Scotland Horse Trials in time for Ian to compete there. A team win in Poland to an individual win in Perth within forty-eight hours was quite something. Thank goodness Sir Wattie was coming home more sedately. With Iain Couttie to look after him he was in good hands but nevertheless very tired after his long journey and ready for a well-earned winter rest at Abbotsford. It is quite amusing to think that this horse has been all round the world in lorries, ferries and 'planes and yet I can vividly remember him as a five year old needing a lot of persuasion to go into his trailer!

Now, with a strong sense of the close of the event season looming up, Ian set off for the three-day event at Chatsworth, with one of his most promising young horses, Kingarth. Leased for the Edinburgh Woollen Mill from our great friend Anne Cranston, we had high hopes that he would go well. With many successes earlier in the year, this gelding showed great potential. Anne and I got down in time for cross-country day and also, sadly, to see him jar himself badly off a drop fence on the hard ground. Having gone well and given Ian a great ride, the horse was unsound after he had finished his round and had heat in a tendon. He couldn't be put forward for the Sunday vetting and in fact had a year off. He is now back into slow work but is a classic example of eventing injuries and strains which however slight need a long time to heal. Although a year may seem an eternity to the rider, it is nothing in the recovery time for a horse.

Meanwhile Ian stayed in the south for the Horse of the Year Show at Olympia. Oxford Blue was required to be there for a parade. With an Australian girl called Gill Jarrett to help me, we pushed him into the trailer in the dark and travelled him down to London during the night when the roads were quiet. At that time I didn't have an H.G.V. licence for the lorry, so car and trailer seemed the obvious alternative. The car was packed to bulging point with our own bags, clothes which Ian had forgotten to take, and all Robbie's tack and gear. Describing it as overloaded was an understatement. Gill almost had to sit on the roof.

The parade involved all our World Championship horses, apart from many others, and it was lovely to see them all looking fit and well together in that floodlit arena. It brought back memories of the prize-giving in Australia in the spring, and it seemed no time at all since then. It was a very fitting moment to retire Priceless from the competitive scene but watching him bouncing round on his lap of honour Ginny had her hands full. Mr P was not an O.A.P. yet! The funniest part of our visit to Olympia was that after we got settled into our hotel room that night the fire alarm went off and hundreds of us had to stand out on the pavement freezing for over an hour. We were probably not a pretty sight for the firemen who discovered it was a false alarm anyway. Clissy Strachan still maintains she could smell burning and see the smoke. She went and spent the rest of the night in her lorry because she was convinced that the firemen were wrong. The rest of us trooped morosely back into the hotel, several sets of pyjamas diverting to the bar. Someone muttered 'This happens every year. I'm not coming out when it goes off next year.'

Ian didn't come home that week but went on out to France to Le Lion d'Angers to ride Yair. This was another of his up-and-coming youngsters and Ian was looking forward to taking him round this French event – his last competition for 1986. I'm afraid I didn't go out and was feeling totally deflated. Responsibilities at home frequently get the better of me and this was one such occasion. Feeling extremely guilty I was very relieved when he 'phoned home each night and seemed fine. Yair behaved and went well and so I didn't feel so bad about not being there to support him.

It was with a tremendous sense of relief that we then took the chance of a holiday in Jamaica. Ian was offered all expenses paid in exchange for competing and teaching out there while I just tagged along. Everyone at home was complaining about the cold whilst we were soaking up the sun. We got very spoilt in the holiday atmosphere and Ian kept saying that when we got home we should just go away for Christmas and New Year as well! So we did. It totalled up as a month away from the telephone which meant peace and quiet and it also meant that Ian got some time for skiing. We took the kids with us on our second holiday to the snow. Both of

Eventing in Jamaica – Ian riding an ex-racehorse Novalis. November 1986.

them show signs of inheriting their father's taste for speed when released on skis! I am not nearly so brave on mine and it has been known for me to shuffle my way round onto a chair lift and as I swing high up into the air my skis are far below me lying in the snow!

1987 and yet another event season seemed quite far away but suddenly we were back into it and making preparations for Badminton. People kept asking Ian if Sir Wattie could win it again. We only had the horses in walking work and our clothes had only

just been put away from our holiday. Ian was busy thinking about talks, courses, lecture-demonstrations, indoor show-jumping and then a different opportunity popped up – the chance to go down south to stay in Gloucestershire for two months at Stowell Park, the home of Lord and Lady Vestey. (It was very much thanks to Henrietta King, Lady Vestey's sister that we got this golden opportunity.) We whizzed down there on a Friday at the end of February to see round the stables and flat which we had so kindly been offered the use of for our stay. At this point Lady Vestey was probably not used to the speed we arranged things and I remember her saying gently, 'Were you meaning to come down here soon?' To which Ian replied, 'Well, yes, Monday if that's O.K.' Rightly, she looked horrified.

It was quite an adventure. We uprooted the kids from school at home, packed up most of our belongings and about eight horses, and moved. Our friends at home thought we had left Scotland for good. It was all just part of the run-up to Badminton. Our first week there went something like this:

Sunday 1st March	Tranwell Team Chase – Jenny at home packing.
Monday 2nd March	Move to Stowell Park – Jenny exhausted.
Tuesday 3rd March	Recovering – horses settling in, kids at new school.
Wednesday 4th March	Ian up at Stoneleigh and evening lecture-demo – Jenny got lost trying to find her way there and had to pick up a hitch-hiker to get put on the correct road!
Thursday 5th March	Ian starting to panic about exam.
Friday 6th March	Ian sits BHSI Stable Manager's exam – lectures Jenny whole way there

OPPOSITE ABOVE Ian's horses in the snow January 1987. (*Left to right*) Griffin, Wattie, Glenburnie, Yair (almost hidden), Charlie Brown and Deerhunter.

OPPOSITE Yair jumping in his characteristic style. Hagley Hall 1987.

Friday	about how it is a *complete* waste of time – then passes! Someone came to see a horse in the afternoon but was more interested in buying Haggis the dog!
Saturday 7th March and Sunday 8th March	Crookham Horse Trials – event season kick off. Cancelled due to bad weather.

Both children were in bed with colds by this time which is probably not surprising, and anyone other than Sandra Miller who was working for us would have left by then. As she was recovering from breaking her pelvis the summer before she ended up doing all the totally unsuitable heavy work about the stables and I did all the slow exercising. When he was there Ian did school the horses. Fortunately another girl from home, Cassy Carruthers, joined us and that took the pressure off us considerably. The only major drama with her was that her horse made repeated attempts at escaping onto Lord Vestey's immaculately kept polo field and it also made up its mind to retire from the competitive life before it even got started. We couldn't complain when Gwen, Cassy's mum had moved in as well and took over our household management. She nursed along ailing children and made sure we had meals rather than living on beans all the time. When she went home she was unwell herself for about six weeks – probably because we had been such a strain to cope with! In fact it never ceases to amaze me that people still actually want to come and stay with us. We live in an organised chaos. You open our desk diary for the week's events and a mass of scribbles and scrawls on the pages hit you. It looks like a heaped up jigsaw puzzle.

There is no doubt at all that we could not manage to keep our hectic schedule going without all those people who lend us a hand. One day everything might grind to a halt when Ian stops competing but in the meantime our life keeps whirling like a merry-go-round. We live from one competition to the next. Everything else slots in around them. Without our fantastic sponsors and friends we couldn't keep going. When Badminton

The launch of the new Equorian tweed to raise money for the 1988 Seoul Olympics and the children and Haggis the dog get in on the act.

An aerial view of Haughhead.

was cancelled in the spring and the rain was bucketing down, I was only grateful that it was Lady Vestey herself who broke the news to Ian. She was every bit as disappointed as he was.

Wherever we are, our house and yard is always a hive of activity. We totally depend on whichever young people are supporting us at the time. One girl spent her whole summer holidays with us this year and worked in return for her keep. I promised her mum that we would try and put her right off horses altogether. I had obviously failed when Marilyn wrote and said thanks for 'the best

Griffin showing his wonderful style during the making of the video *Horse Riding*, summer 1987.

holiday I've ever had!' We never encourage young people to stay with us more than a year but while they do they live as family and get landed with every job that's going. They have to learn to drive if they can't do that already and as well as grooming they get cooking and babysitting. The first boy who worked for us, George Graham, used to have his lunch with a baby in a high chair on each side of him. I can still hear him saying, 'One to you, one to me, one to you' as he stuffed spoonfulls of food into babies and himself. Anyone who comes to work or train with Ian really has to like children,

109

especially now they are school age, miss nothing and are frequently quite critical. Ian was lungeing Yair one day and must have looked most intent. Tim's comment in the car as he was driven past was, 'There's Daddy tying a horse in a knot again' which was probably exactly what Ian felt like doing!

It's not only the children's comments that make us laugh and keep us going. The teenagers who stay with us come out with some good ones as well. We were discussing the title of this book and Ian protested that he doesn't do everything fast. He had finished his lunch and the rest of us were still eating. Iain Graham piped up, 'Ian says he's slowed down. The car was shuddering the other day and he was doing 120mph. What was he like before?'

Well, perhaps we should ask his mum, to whom we owe so much. After all, Ian was nearly born in the taxi before she could get into the hospital!

Afterthought

1987 came to a close with a tremendous trip out to Lühmühlen, to the European Championships, with Sir Wattie. This horse is an incredible trier and could not have done better than his second place to Night Cap, the deserving winner. It was team gold and individual silver medals for Ian, thanks to Wattie who never gave his rider a rough moment on the extremely testing cross-country course. There had been several falls, not least Lucinda Green's spectacular one on Shannagh but they got up and finished their round, much to their credit. Jane Thelwall had a fight with a tree near the end of her round and not surprisingly came off worst. On show-jumping morning the British Squad could boast that they had the most unsound riders. Jane was in agony with her bruised knee and Captain Mark Phillips had a leg that would have failed any vet's inspection.

The show-jumping was rather a tense day as it can always tend to be so there was great hilarity afterwards when Lucinda went and rode in the races on draught horses. These huge farm animals had been brought in for the afternoon and she and Eddy Stibbe, the international Dutch rider, had a go at setting the heavy horses alight! Raymond Brooks-Ward, the BBC commentator, also nearly went up in smoke when he received an electric shock from his microphone which turned live halfway through his interview with the team. As he jumped about four feet in the air we only hoped this would be televised at home because it would have been impossible to do an action replay!

LÜHMÜHLEN 1987

BELOW Checking the going in the water was colder than it looked.

OPPOSITE ABOVE A study of concentration. Sir Wattie.

OPPOSITE BELOW Wattie making life look easy.

LÜHMÜHLEN 1987

BELOW Looking confident and happy at the final vet's inspection.

OPPOSITE ABOVE LEFT Wattie showjumping.

OPPOSITE ABOVE RIGHT Britain 1st and 2nd with Germany's Claus Erhorn 3rd.

OPPOSITE BELOW Victorious team – Lühmühlen European Championships 1987. (*Left to right*) Lucinda Green, Rachel Hunt, Ginny Leng and Ian.

As Ginny and Hamish Leng drove us along to the airport on the Monday morning and flew back to London with us, our thoughts were turning to Burghley, just around the corner. Neither of the riders in the car could have been looking forward to their prospective rides at the British event just as much as the ones they had had out in Germany. Both Night Cap and Sir Wattie had just demonstrated their skills and experience. Ian knew he was about to compete with Yair who had neither of these, in comparison. As it turned out Ginny withdrew Master Craftsman and before we knew it we had arrived at Burghley with Yair. High as a kite on dressage day, Ian just hoped Yair would concentrate on his cross-country. As it happened he didn't and gave Ian a crashing fall at the sixth fence, the Burghley Bridge. Ian said he had changed his mind about where to ride the fence but now that we have watched the video replay many times in our house we are all agreed that it was the horse that made a mistake, probably due to lack of experience. As a result he actually went much better on the rest of his round and gave Ian a very good ride on the remainder of the course. Too late, the damage was done. The Sunday morning saw Ian at the vet's inspection on crutches even though his horse trotted up sound. Yair had seen to it that Ian didn't stay on a high too long after winning medals in Germany. What is it they say about horses being great levellers?

The 1987 season however was to finish on a high note for us when we heard that Ian had won the British points championship with a total of 637 points.

As we check the final proofs of this book it is mid-winter and already we are looking forward eagerly to the new season ahead of us. Who knows what it will bring.

OPPOSITE Interesting style – Yair at Burghley 1987.

ABOVE A rare moment of relaxation for the four of us.

The Equine Stars

Sir Wattie

Jointly owned by Edinburgh Woollen Mill and Dame Jean Maxwell-Scott
By Bronze Hill (T.B.) out of Rosa (Hunter Mare)

1983   1st Fenton OI – Ian's first win higher than novice.
1st Bramham three-day event (Standard). Ian's first three-day event win, Wattie's first three-day event.
2nd Achselschwang CCI (Germany). Ian's first overseas trip. Member of winning team with Lorna Clarke, Liz Kershaw. Long listed for Olympics.

1984   6th Badminton CCI. Ian's first ride round Badminton.
Reserve horse to Oxford Blue for Los Angeles Olympics.
3rd Scottish Championships, Thirlestane. Top Scottish horse and rider.

1985   Off for the year with bruised tendon sheath.

1986   1st Badminton. Ian's first and 'to date' only win there.
1st Scottish Championships, Open.
3rd Poland CCIO. Member of winning team with Ginny Leng, Rachel Hunt and Madeleine Gurdon.

1987   Badminton cancelled.
European Championships, Luhmühlen, Germany.
Member of winning team with Ginny Leng, Rachel Hunt and Lucinda Green. Individual Silver.

Oxford Blue

On loan from Miss E. Davidson
By Cagirama (T.B.) out of Blewberry Fair (T.B.)

1983   3rd Bramham three-day event (Standard); Robbie's first three-day event.
7th Boekelo CCI (Holland). Winning team with Lucinda

Green, Tiny Clapham and Lizzie Purbrick.
Long listed for the Olympics.

1984   3rd Badminton – Ian's first year at Badminton.
2nd Olympic final trial – Castle Ashby.
9th Los Angeles Olympics – Silver team medal with
Ginny Leng, Lucinda Green and Tiny Clapham. Ian's
first official team and first and only Olympics (to date).

1985   21st Badminton – due to a fall at the Quarry.
Individual Bronze Medalist at European championships,
Burghley. Member of gold medal team with Ginny
Leng, Lucinda Green and Lorna Clarke.

1986   11th Individual at World championship (Australia) (fell
on the flat). Gold team medal winner with Ginny Leng,
Lorna Clarke and Clissy Strachan.
Retired from eventing after Australian trip.

Hunted all season 1986/87, then ran in two hunter chases in
March 1987. Unplaced, but horse and rider had a great time.
Now, 1987/88 season, being hunted by Lady Vestey with the
Beaufort Hunt.

Charlie Brown IV

On loan from Mrs H. Whitson
By Zara Crackle (T.B.) out of a pony/mare

1984   1st Bramham three-day event. Charlie Brown's first
three-day event.

1985   9th Chatsworth three-day event.

1986   20th approx Luhmühlen CCI. Fell in show jumping.
Member of the winning Commonwealth team, with
Lucinda Green and Mark Todd (NZ).

1987   1st Weston Park. Advanced level.
4th Brigstock. Advanced level.
1st Belton Park. Advanced level.
2nd Stowell Park. Advanced level.

Glenburnie

Owned by Edinburgh Woollen Mill
By Precipice Wood (T.B.) out of a thoroughbred mare

1985   1st Scottish Championships. Novice.
2nd British Championships. Novice.
11th Chatsworth three-day event. Glenburnie's first
three-day event.

1986   10th after dressage at Badminton then withdrew due to
deep going.
4th Le Touquet CCI (France). Winning team with
Ginny Leng, Richard Walker and Clissy Strachan.
4th Burghley CCI.

1987   1st Brigstock. Advanced level.
Badminton cancelled.
Shortlisted for European championships but leg injury
forced rest for remainder of year.

Kingarth

On loan from Miss Anne Cranston
By Bronze Hill out of a Connemara Cross

1986   1st Belton Park. Advanced level.

Yair

Owned by Edinburgh Woollen Mill
By Bivouac (T.B.) out of a hunter mare

1986   1st Scottish Championships, Novice.
10th Le Lion D'Angers CCI (France). Yair's first three-
day event.

1987   3rd Witton Castle, Advanced level.
12th Bramham three-day event.
3rd Scottish Championships, Open.
Now sold to David Bartram

Bridge The Gap

On loan from Mr and Mrs A. Kershaw
By Casterbridge (Irish T.B.)

1987   4th Rowallan Castle. His first Advanced event.
5th Chatsworth CCI. His first three-day event.
Now sold to Germany

Griffin

Owned by Edinburgh Woollen Mill
By Near Cottage Pearl out of Mega Flash (T.B.)

1987   4th Eglinton. Griffin's first advanced event.
1st Gatcombe Park. Advanced level.

Deansland

On short term loan from Mrs G. Short
By Cagirama out of Ladhope (Hunter Mare)

1985   1st Charterhall OI. Ian's first ride on this horse.
1st Bramham three-day event.
Shortlisted for European Championships, Burghley.
5th Final Trial Locko Park.

Now returned to his owner (loaned whilst she was having a baby!)

Up and Coming Novices

Mix'N Match

Owned by Edinburgh Woollen Mill.
Six-year-old piebald gelding by Tudor Diver (T.B.).
Now Intermediate.

Set Sail

On loan from Mrs Barbara Slane-Fleming, Ian's dressage trainer.
Six-year-old bay gelding, Irish Bred.

The Designer

Owned by Edinburgh Woollen Mill.
Six-year-old brown gelding by Smooth Stepper (Irish T.B.).

Index

Abbotsford 65, 96, 101
Achselschwang 34–5, 119
Alnwick 30
Andeguy 37, 38
Anne, H.R.H. Princess 72–3, 93
Ashkirk 52, 53, 54
Australia 64, 66, 75, 78–86, 120

Babu, J. J. 95
Badminton 30, 32, 38–42, 58, 64,
    66–77, 92, 93, 103, 105, 106,
    119, 120, 121
Barley, Susie 79
Barr, Sam 22
Bartram, David 121
Beaufort, Duchess of 39
  Duke of 39, 93
  Hunt 120
Belton Park 66, 120, 121
Ben Rinnes 56
Beresford, Lord Patrick 80, 99
Bialy Bor 98
Bivouac 121
Black Magic 12, 13
Blewberry Fair 119
Blue 27
Blue Horizon 13
Boekeolo 36–8, 119
Boyle, Will 9, 10, 12, 13, 14, 15
Bramham 32, 58–9, 119, 120, 121,
    122
Bridge the Gap 122

Brigstock 66, 120, 121
British Horse Society 17, 33
Bronze Hill 28, 119, 121
Brooks-Ward, Raymond 44, 111
Broomhill Farm 12
Brown, Mionie 78
Bruce family 78
Bunny 65
Burgess, Pat 44
Burghley 55–6, 60, 92, 95, 97–8,
    116, 120, 121, 122

Cagirama 27, 119, 122
Campbell, Sarah 41
Carruthers, Cassy 106
  Gwen 106
Casterbridge 122
Castle Ashby 120
Charisma 81, 85, 86
Charlie Brown IV 30–1, 33, 40, 56,
    61, 62, 91–3, 104, 105, 120
Charlie Riddell-Webster 24
Charterhall 29, 122
Chatsworth 61–3, 101, 120, 121,
    122
Cholderton 65
Christie, Stuart 73
Clapham, Tiny 37, 46, 47, 48, 50,
    90, 120
Clarke, Lorna 30, 34, 35, 36, 38, 60,
    78, 80, 81, 82, 84, 85, 119, 120
Claughton Horse Trials 30

Comerford, Marjorie 37
Connemara Cross 121
Corbridge 18
Couttie, Iain 64, 66, 82, 87, 88, 89, 92, 93, 101
Cranston, Anne 12, 18, 32, 66, 93, 95, 101, 121
  Bob 18
  Margaret 12, 13, 18
Crookham 106

Dalmahoy Horse Trials 30
Davidson, Bruce 95
  Liz 27, 39, 41, 49, 119
Davies, Claire 7, 32, 38, 41, 45, 66, 71, 78, 82
Deansland 56, 58, 59, 65, 122
Deerhunter 104, 105
Delphy Dazzle 60, 84, 85
Dryden 17, 20, 28

Edgar, Ted 49
Edinburgh Woollen Mill 7, 43, 67, 72, 75-7, 96, 101, 119, 121, 122, 123
Eglinton 30, 92, 122
Eilberg, Ferdi 44, 83
Erhorn, Claus 114-15
Ettrick Forest Riders'
    Association 17
  Riding Club 18, 20

FEI 33
Fenton 18, 119
Fergus of Dryden 22
Finvarra 84, 86
Fleischman, Torrance 84, 86
Foxy 94
France *see* Le Lion d'Angers, Le
    Touquet

Galashiels 9, 24
Gallant Lad 18
Gamesmaster 46, 48
Gatcombe 59, 93, 95, 122
Gawler 64, 65, 81-6
Germany *see* Achselschwang,
    Lühmühlen

Glenburnie 61, 62, 63, 64, 65, 67, 75, 87, 88, 89, 92, 93, 95, 96, 97, 98, 104, 105, 121
Glenmoidart 15, 16, 18
Good News 61
Gordon-Watson, Mary 90
Graham, George 109
  Iain 110
Green, David 45, 60
  Lucinda 37, 41, 46, 47, 48, 49, 50, 60, 68, 92, 111, 114-15, 119, 120
Greenhill 20, 57
Greyfriars Bobby 17
Greyfriars Lass 17, 18-20
Griffin 104-5, 109, 122
Gurdon, Madeleine 60, 100, 119

Hagley Hall 104, 105
Harrison, Charles 37
Haughhead 22, 23, 54, 58, 75, 108
Hawick 12
Haynes, Colin 82
Hennig, Gavin 90-3, 97
Higham, Brian 75
Hogarth, Tony 20
Holgate, Heather 46, 84, 87, 89, 100
  Virginia *see* Leng
Holland *see* Boekeolo
Hong Kong 79
Hope, Chris 82
Horse of the Year Show 101-2
Hughes, Bill 24, 25, 28
Hunt, Rachel 72, 100, 114-15, 119

Indian Tonic 17, 18-19
Innes, Fanny 17, 18-19
Inverurie 22

Jamaica 64, 102-3
Jarrett, Gill 101
Jet Set 37
Joicey family 18
Jonjo 94
Just the Thing 35
Justin Thyme 84

Keay, Errol 21

125

Kershaw, Alwyn   34, 122
  Liz   34, 35, 36, 119, 122
King, Henrietta   105
Kingarth   65, 66, 93, 95, 101, 121

Ladhope   10, 122
Lairdstown   56, 58
Laub, Barbara   22
Langholm   75-7
Le Lion d'Angers   102, 121
Le Touquet   87-90, 121
Lemieux, Robert   46, 48
Leng, Hamish   84, 116
  (née Holgate), Virginia ('Ginny')
    46, 47, 48, 50, 55, 60, 78, 80,
    81, 82, 83, 84, 85, 86, 87, 89,
    90, 99, 100, 102, 114-15, 116,
    119, 120, 121
Linsey Park Stud   81-2
Lochore, Pollyann   27, 56
Locko Park   30, 33, 59, 122
Luczyc-Wyhowska, Susan   28, 68,
  96
Lühmühlen   90-3, 111-16, 119, 120

McAulay, Catriona   17
  ('Granny') Jean   7, 17, 18
  Jenny *see* Stark
McGlashan, Susan   36
Machattie, Norah   27
Maitland-Carew family   96
  Rosi   61
Mardon, Sheila   22
  Shuna   30
Master Adam   20
Master Craftsman   116
Maxwell-Scott, Dame Jean   28, 48,
  52, 65, 68, 96, 119
Meade, Richard   37, 38
Mega Flash   122
Melrose   14
Miller, Sandra   66, 68, 91, 106
Mix 'N Match   123
Murphy   89, 90
Myross   60, 84, 85

Near Cottage Pearl   122
New Zealand   56-7, 81, 86

Night Cap   48, 55, 99, 111, 116
Nobilin   24, 25
Novalis   103

Olympics
  Los Angeles, 1984   38, 43-54,
    119, 120
  Seoul, 1988   107
Orchard, Mandy   78
Osberton   61
Oseman, Claire   90
Oxford Blue (Robbie)   26-7, 30, 32,
    36, 37, 38, 39, 40, 41, 45, 47,
    48, 49, 50, 58, 60, 64, 65, 66,
    78, 84, 85, 86, 87, 101, 119-20

Perth   101
Philip, H.R.H. Prince   80
Phillips, Captain Mark   93, 95, 111
Piglet   100
Pinnacle   78
Piper Heidsieck   78
Poland   92, 98-100, 119
Pomeroy   60
Pony Club   15
Pottinger, Tinks   86
Powell, Rodney   60, 99
Precipice Wood   121
Priceless   46, 48, 60, 85, 86, 102
Pukekohe   56
Purbrick, Lizzie   37, 120
Pybus, Edward   61

Quarter Horse   30
Queen, H.M. The   40
Queenie   62

Regal Realm   47, 49, 60
Riding Club   16, 17, 18, 29
Rippon, Angela   75
Robbie *see* Oxford Blue
Rodger, Jackie   15, 16, 17, 21, 24
Rosa   119
Rosie   28
Rowallan Castle   122
Royal Highland Show   27
Royal International Horse Show   45
Russell, Lady Hugh   37, 43, 44

Sandys-Lumsdaine, Leesa   53
Scott-Dunn, Peter   59, 84
Scott-Plummer family   16
  Joan   18
Sederholm, Lars   36
Selkirk   12, 13, 94
Set Sail   123
Shannagh   48, 111
Short, Ann   59, 122
Sir Wattie   26–30, 32, 34, 35, 38, 39,
    40, 41, 45, 48, 55, 56, 58, 60,
    63, 64, 65, 67–77, 93, 95–6, 98,
    101, 103, 104, 105, 111, 112–
    13, 114–15, 116, 119
Slane-Fleming, Barbara   7, 43, 68,
    123
Slater, Jean   21, 52
Smith, Les   54
Smokey Shane   57
Smooth Stepper   123
Spence, Andrew   27
SR Direct Mail   75
Stark, Derek   9
  Ian
    boyhood   9–12
    school   12
    early teens   12–15
    leaves school   15, 17
    begins competing   15–16
    DHSS office job   17
    begins dressage   17–18
    courting and marriage   20–2
    children   22–3
    leaves DHSS   26
    learning to fly   32
    1983: the turning point,
        Bramham   32
      Germany   34–5
      Holland   36–8
    1984: Badminton   38–42
      sponsorship starts   43
      Olympics, Los
        Angeles   43–54
      British points
        championship   56
      New Zealand   56–7
    1985: Badminton   58
      Bramham   58–9

Locko Park   59
Burghley   55–6, 60
Chatsworth   61–3
1986: Badminton   66–77
  Australia   78–86
  France   87–90
  Germany   92–3
  Gatcombe   93–5
  Thirlestane Castle   96
  Burghley   97–8
  Poland   98–100
  Perth   101
  Chatsworth   101
  Horse of the Year
    Show   101–2
  France   102
1987: Badminton cancelled   108
  Germany   111
  Burghley   116
  British points
    championship   116
(née McAulay) Jenny   57, 62
  background   17
  marriage   22
  and *passim*
Linda   9
('Granny') Pearl   7, 9, 10, 12, 52,
    62, 78, 87, 110
Stephanie   23, 52, 54, 55, 62, 63,
    66, 77, 94, 95, 102–3, 106
Tim   23, 62, 77, 102–3, 106, 110
Steinler, Barbara and Theo   35
Stevenson, Alix   7, 72, 75
  David   7, 43, 72, 73, 75–7, 95–6
Stibbe, Eddy   111
Stive, Karen   47
Stoneleigh   17, 20, 105
Stowell Park   105, 120
Strachan, Clarissa ('Clissy')   60, 78,
    80, 82, 84, 85, 90, 102, 120, 121
Sugar   62
Sunderland Hall   16, 18

Taimur   35
Taylor, Anne-Marie   78, 82, 84
The Designer   123
The Done Thing   60, 100
The Grousebeater   37

Thelwall, Jane   99, 111
Thirlestane   62, 95, 119
Thompson, Lucy   90
Todd, Mark   65, 79, 80, 81, 86, 92, 120
Tucker, Mike   97
Tudor Diver   123

Vestey, Lady   105, 108, 120
   Lord   105
Village Gossip   37
Volunteer   86
VSOP   59

Walker, Richard   90, 121
Wallace, Major Malcolm   46, 53, 80
Wares family   90
Weldon, Frank   93

Weston Park   120
Whitbread Trophy   73
Whitehead, Pat   53
Whitson, Harold   92
   Rowena   40, 92, 120
Willis, Dot   84
Willis brothers   93
Wilson, Ann   57
Windjammer   46, 47
Witton Castle   121
Wooden, Kelso   30
Woodside Dreamer   21, 22, 30
Wylye   21, 43, 44, 45, 56, 65, 66, 93

Yair   65, 102, 104, 105, 110, 116–17, 121

Zara Crackle   120